GOD IS ME

The path to enlightenment through self reflection

A collection of notes and reflections on connecting to your inner spiritual guide, written by Grigoria Kritsotelis

DEDICATION

To God, for all that I am, all that I have and all that I am becoming, and for working through me in this way.

To my parents, for allowing me to be exactly who I desire to be and providing a sacred safe space for me to grow up in.

To my sister, for always supporting my woo woo tangents and embracing the woo woo life.

To Moey, for not quite getting it, but supporting me regardless.

To Danayra, for seeing my value even before I saw it myself.

To Gahmya, for being my forever teacher.

To Ms P, for supporting my writing in Year 10 English and for keeping my essays all those years later.

And to all of you, for embracing who YOU are and allowing me to be on this journey with you.

I love you.

CONTENTS

FOREWORD

Written by Gahmya Drummond Bey

What's your earliest memory? Mine is crystal clear. I am two years old in my earliest memory. I am sitting in a stroller and listening to my parents argue, as I watch droplets of water fall into a bucket. I feel incredibly calm and surprisingly strong. I feel invincible. I have only one thought- 'How can I fix this?" There was not an ounce of doubt that I would be able to fix things. It was more a question of the certain way that I would do it. At two years old, I felt like a superhero.

The thing is, the question, "How can I fix this" has been a mainstay throughout my life. As a global curriculum designer, "How can I fix this" has helped me to travel the world and redesign learning in over thirty countries. But, I'm not always confident. There are times when I question if I can "fix" things or even if my "fixing" things has done more harm than good. But, it's in those moments that I have to remember the two year old me in that stroller. That two year old came here with a purpose gripped tightly in her little hands and didn't doubt it one bit. She knew who she was. But, we all forget

8

who we are and that's why we need people like Grigoria to remind us.

When I first met Grigoria, we were both being interviewed in a series for Women Entrepreneurs around the world. We were in different countries, but her energy was (and continues to be) magnetic. One of the most powerful things Grigoria has ever said to me was, "Remember who you are. You are God in flesh." It's a reminder that we all need as we continue upon our journey of self-remembering and stepping into our greatest possibility. How much differently would you treat yourself if you moved with the constant awareness that you were walking around in God's body? Feeding God's body? Exercising or neglecting God's body? How much better would we all speak to ourselves?

It took the longest time for me to create a morning practice that stuck. I would read something inspiring and become excited about building a new habit, and then, my excitement would vanish. However, the thought of being in God's body reminded me that if I would simply surrender, and navigate my life with the confidence of that two year old, all would unfold beautifully.

Grigoria's words are like that. They stick with you. She's deeply connected and channels from her connection to the

Divine to yours and you know it because she energises you. She acts as a mirror, showing you your possibility.

This book is Grigoria's light dancing in ink. The essence is of pure love, guiding you along the way. As you read, imagine your best self waiting on the last page, hand extended just eager for you to grasp and hold on. Eager for you to remember who you are and who you have always been.

Gahmya Drummond-Bey
Conscious Education Expert
Founder: Evolvedteacher
Author: The Life of Ideas

INTRODUCTION

Things to be assumed as you journey through this book: When I make reference to "God", I am referring to God/ Universe/Angels/source/infinite intelligence/energy/whatever your truth is.

There is no beginning, middle or end to this book. It is a series of reflections, in much the same way as my mind works; sporadically. I have created a collection of reflections, notes and ideas that ultimately altered my physical experience. They have led me here, sharing my thoughts with you. And it is by no accident that you have stumbled upon this book. It will resonate with the deepest parts of you, and it is YOU who will give the words meaning. My intentions for the meaning of this book do not hold as much significance as your perception of the words written here. God has worked through me to deliver this message, but the message is yours, and it's through your own experience that anything written here will hold any value at all. You will find what you seek to find.

The premise of this book is that I may not be God, but God is me. God is all of us. Collectively we come from God, and to God we shall return. And that truth means that if we believe that we come from the infinite supply, the infinite energy source, then we too believe that we harness and embody it's Divine power to be, do and create all things. Your Divinity is absolute. The only thing that waivers is your belief in that truth. I'm here to guide you to remember.

Together we declare, I, as an individualisation of God, am not all of God, but God is all of me. As I write these words, God flows through me. This is my creative expression where my soul longs to be received and perceived. I translate the channeled angels in the best way I can so that prayers are answered through the messages. I too, long to receive your expressions, so that my prayers can be answered through you. This book isn't about what words I'm channeling, as much as it's about what you interpret the words to mean to you. Use the power you find within these pages. Your message is important. In fact, it is integral, without you, we are not whole.

— — — — — —

CHAPTER 1

THE SALVATION OF THE HEALER

I am healed because I am the healer. I am healed because I am the healer, I repeated to myself, over and over again. Some may say that by using such a statement I'm not showing my faith in God… Whereas I see it as proof of my unwavering faith in God because I am acknowledging my ability to co-create *with* God. I recognise my own Divinity - the divinity bestowed upon me *from* God. The same divinity bestowed upon everyone. Because in fact, God works through me. So I'll say it again - I am healed because I am the healer. I am healed because I am the healer.

Revelations from my soul:

I am the one. I repeat to myself over and over again in my mind. I am the one. My truth is my own and it does not need to align with your truth. My truth isn't THE truth, but my truth is very real to me. And my truth determines how I think, feel and perceive my reality, thus our realities will all vary because they are dependent on our own truths. I know that I am the one. It doesn't matter what that means, it also doesn't matter if others believe that about themselves too or even if I am not the one. What matters is that I know I'm the one. And in my knowing I emit a different sort of frequency, one that doesn't quiver with a glimpse of doubt, because in my knowing lives an indescribable power. A power that lives in harmony with the song of the Universe, a power that can create or destroy all things. I have found the perfect harmony. I have been trying to sing along with the Universe my whole life. Trying to understand what it truly means to be one with the Universe, because of course I am the entire Universe and the entire Universe is me. But to say, to think, to feel and to believe do not compare to the knowing. I now know. I know I am the one. I know I encompass all the power. I know that I write my own dream. This life isn't for me, it's from me. And all the things I believed I wanted, all the people, all the experiences, I now realise that I have them all already. And they live in the knowing. They were always there, but I didn't know that then. But now I do. They all exist because I know they exist. If I didn't know, then they don't exist. So I ask you, do you know who you are? The knowing comes from your relationship with source. So your first step is to understand your relationship with source. You come from it, so whatever God has the power to create, you can co-create with Him. The second part comes from your understanding of the human conditioning of this physical realm and how it has clouded your knowing. Once you are aware you regain all your power. Because it is in our awareness that we have the power to change. If we aren't aware, we do not know that there needs to be a change, or that we even have a choice.

PRAYER

Thank you God. Thank you. Thank you. Thank you. Thank you. Thank you. The only words I ever really need to pray. Thank you for all that I am, all that I have and all that I am becoming. Thank you for this experience. Thank you for using me as a vessel. Thank you for spreading your message through me. Thank you for showing me the way. Thank you for guiding me. Thank you for the way you love me. True love isn't my love for you, but your love for me. It is there where I find what it truly means to love unconditionally. Even in my imperfection, you find my infinite perfection. Even in my mistrials, you see me as I truly am. Pure light. And it makes sense, you see me as I truly am because I am your manifestation. And you created me in your own perfect image. And my job here is to experience all of this. And there is nothing more required of me. I am to love and to feel joy. There is more than enough time. There is more than enough of everything. It is impossible for me to get it wrong. How would it be possible if you work through me. It isn't possible. And all I ever have to remember is who I truly am. I am light. I am love. I am the stars above. And I am the earth below. I am you. And you are me. I am everyone. And everyone is me. I feel you. Thank you God. Thank you. Thank you. Thank you. Thank you. Thank you. Thank you. I love you.

-

THE SALVATION OF THE HEALER

Sometimes I hear whispers, whispers from a world far beyond this one. Whispers from the version of me that still lives in the stars. The me that lives in the place of holiness, the holiness I sometimes forget exists within me here. But those whispers are not whispers of words. But instead whispers of moments. The light breeze brushing over my cheeks. The Godly sun kissing my chest. The stems of grass bedding themselves under my feet. The angelic smile from the child walking past. Or the salty lick of my dogs tongue against my arm. It's in these moments that I feel completely connected to the Divine. That I remember where I came from and what I'm here to do. It's in these moments that I am present. And being present in each moment allows me to feel everything and nothing all at once. The moments past and the moments to come are just thoughts, this moment is the only reality that exists. And it's in this moment that I encompass all the power to create. As I am unable to create in the past and I am unable to create in the future. It's only now that I can create. And my creation right now will determine my vibration and my vibration will determine my ability to create in the next moment. So it's in this moment that I hold all my power. So my desire to create is dependent on how present I am right now. And so I focus on how I feel right now, and that realisation leads me to a choice - I get to choose how I feel right now. So my choice becomes my feeling, which becomes my vibration, which determines my ability to create. The flow feels so easy. So other-worldly. It's all from within. All of it. As above, so below, as within, so without. So to have anything, worldly or unworldly, I must first look within.

And what happened when I set my soul free..? And by set free I mean releasing the conditions of this physical world and unlearning everything I was taught so I can truly be free... I was able to truly fall in love with life and feel it. Feel the joy of each moment. And I really mean the joy. The joy in the afternoon traffic, the joy in tripping over, the joy in the sand between my toes and the joy in my sister's smile. And that joy allowed God to flow through me freely. Imagine uncovering the secret of the Universe. I had the light switch which could turn on God at any time. But that's not really the secret. The secret is that the light is ALWAYS on, but somehow, through our conditioning and our unconsciousness we seem to believe that it is dark and that darkness makes us believe that we need to *find* the light switch, that we may not be worthy of finding it, that only the select few can turn on the light. Even questioning if the light exists at all. All the while missing the fact that the light is on for all of us at all times. And we invest so much of our energy in finding the switch, we search the most remote places on earth, we believe that only some know how to harness the power, and of those who happened to "find" the switch, only some could flip it. But that's the conditioning of the new age spiritual world - those who have found a way to again instil fear in the minds of the vulnerable. There's more ego than we know what to do with, and it can feel as though we are drowning in the ego. And the air seems too far away. But we have gills. And when we trust ourselves and identify ourselves as who we truly are, then we awaken. Awaken to our own salvation. I am healed as I am the healer. And this level of self actualisation allows God to work through us in unquestionable ways. Once I acknowledge that I am the saviour, I allow God to save me. And through this salvation, all wounds are healed, all pains are forgotten and all trials have passed.

The only reason you aren't living the life you want to be living, seeing the people you want to be seeing or embracing the person you are is because you see separation between you and what is outside of you in this physical realm. Our sacred truth suggests that everything that you desire, everything that you are, is within you. Your salvation is within you. You are your own saviour. Once you come to understand that there is no separation between you and God, you'll come to understand that the salvation you seek, was there, inside of you all along. That's the thing, as said in A Course in Miracles, God wants you to be healed, so He has kept the source of healing where the need of healing lies. My salvation comes from me, nothing outside of me can hold me back. Within me is the world's salvation and my own. This quote sums it up, "the victim mindset dilutes the human potential, by not accepting personal responsibility for our circumstances, we greatly reduce our power to change them." You see so many people around you trying to find fulfilment outside of themselves, in a partner, in other people, in possessions, in achievements, in titles, but upon reflection, those people still feel emptiness. It's like a cup wants to sit in a bath of water and feel full. You'll feel surrounded, but you'll never feel full. So how are you to be your own salvation…? Start by adding good things to your life, one at a time, then over time that pile of good things will grow. And only you can decide what feels good. Little has to change for your whole life to change. Alter your perception and your life will transform. It is already the life you dream of, just believe it is. God works through us. We are delivering important messages. You are not a small part in the web, you are an INTEGRAL part. You live in a world where tomorrow, literally everything can change. You get to decide. You get to choose salvation. And what you allow is what will continue.

If I am of the infinite source, as is everything and everyone, then I can also assume that everything and everyone is yearning to love me, to have me win, to have me realise all of my desires. Just as I wouldn't intentionally wound myself or put myself in harms way or cause myself pain - everything and everyone, whom are my mirrors, wouldn't either. The world is rigged in your favour - always wanting what you want - because why wouldn't I want me? Why wouldn't I want to realise that which is just an extension of me? What you want, wants you too.

AFFIRMATION

What I want is as close as I let it be, and right now I see it here now.

Love and hate cannot exist simultaneously, just as faith and fear cannot exist simultaneously. And so to move forward in faith and to encompass all that you are, we must create moments throughout each day in which we remind ourselves that we are love. We aren't in love, we ARE love. And hate is the absence of love, and fear is the absence of faith, and darkness is the absence of light (or resistance to it). So in each moment you make a decision to move closer to love or further from it. Our natural state of being is love, so there is nothing more required of you to feel it and fully embrace it. When you feel pain, fear, anger, hate, frustration, doubt, it is as though you are trying with all your might to pull away from love. Imagine that you are in the frequency of love, you are there present, it is easy and freeing. And now you decide to doubt that you are there, you question if it's there at all, so you tie a band to yourself and run with all your might away from it, and that path seems difficult, because it's not your natural state of being. You are resisting what is natural, and so it doesn't feel good. And if you were to just surrender to your resistance, you would sling shot back to love. And to surrender is to remove resistance, and that can be as easy as letting go of the thoughts that don't feel good.

But I acknowledge that we experience contrast and often we find ourselves resisting that contrast, as though we have forgotten that we chose contrast because it's in the contrast that we expand. Like the waves in the ocean we ebb and flow through life. Sometimes we show up in the most exceptional way, we allow the world and other people to observe our flow. We bloom and flourish in our own poetic chaos. We overflow with love, with substance, with life. We give to life more than life could ever give to us. And sometimes we show up to ourselves... To the world we retreat, we show up to ourselves with love, with kindness, with gentleness. We ebb, we fill up, we recharge. You see, we are cyclical creatures, and just as we follow moon cycles, sun cycles and earth cycles, our life is too a series of cycles. Old lessons come back to teach us something new, old wounds reopen to teach us how to heal once more. Both the ebb and the flow are just as profound and just as important. Like the waves in the ocean, we must allow ourselves to fill up the cracks and carpet the world with love. As well as to retreat, to allow the world to give to us, to fill us up, to refuel. One is not of greater importance than the other. Actually they only exist because of each other. Honour how you feel, honour the ebb and honour the flow. Honour where you are in the midst of the ebb and flow. Eckhart Tolle says, "accept then act, whatever the present moment contains, accept it as if you had chosen it, always work with it, not against it", happiness is not somewhere else, it is where you are.

We all have areas in our life which feel harder, but all it means is that you may have to work slightly harder to help it flow. You get to decide if your goals will happen someday down the track when the time is right OR if they will start to happen right now because you're making the time right. No one is coming to save you. You are in complete control. And I want today to be your Day One! And let's just say that you completely screw it all up (impossible because everything is a learning experience but for the sake of this story and our human-level of understanding, let's say you completely bomb out), then tomorrow will be Day One again. You are loved. You are supported. You have everything you need. I will not die with regrets. I will live my full life. I will do everything I desire to do. I am comfortable facing my fear. I am willing to do the work and take action. Feed your mind these powerful thoughts and live as though they are your religion. I love you. I see you. I am you.

During a Sacred Shamanic Cacao Ceremony, in which we were in a meditative state for 3 and a half hours, I had a vision about this chapter, and at the end of the ceremony when we shared our experience with the collective, I spoke on how I always believed that this chapter was about helping others heal themselves, and it wasn't until I was in a state of complete surrender (during deep meditation) that I realised, that in fact I was writing this chapter to help heal myself. And that would in turn help heal you. Because you are my reflection, and as I heal myself, I too, heal the whole world. And it's not that I have something specific that I desire to heal, but I do want to feel like myself as often as I can. That is, feel like love. Feel like the energy that I came from, the energy that I am, the energy that I will always be. And I will not let my (conditional) ego cloud my reflection. And I will never take for granted the profoundness of these words, because as I write them here, believing that they are from me, for me, I simultaneously know that I am writing them from you, for you, because we are Divinely connected, and as you have asked for guidance, you are receiving. And I have no doubt that there will be many of you, who reach out to me sharing your stories, your deepest thoughts and your own reflections, which will be answers to questions I have asked in which God chose you as a vessel to deliver those messages to me. It's no small feat being human; experiencing this physical world, feeling all the feelings, remembering who we are, and making our way home. But I wouldn't have it any other way. Because right now, I know I'm exactly where I'm supposed to be, and I am ready for what I am ready for, and right now, YOU are ready for this, and as I talk to you, I talk to myself. But note, that the answers may not be in the words, they will be in the feelings the words give you. Just like art, this is my creative expression, wanting to make you feel something. And if it doesn't feel good, it's not the truth, because the only truth is love, and so the only feeling that will resonate with our Divine truth, is that of love and well-being. Listen to your inner guide, she is always talking to you, she never shouts, she never forces, she whispers and she flows.

The God Switch…

Let's talk about the God Switch. During another Sacred Cacao Shamanic Ceremony, I found myself on a slightly different journey. This time, I went deep fast. And all of a sudden I found myself completely connected to Source, as in "The Source". The all-knowing, infinite intelligence, every-thought-ever-thought kind of Source. And at first I questioned my place there. I needed "proof" that I was really there. So I asked the big ticket question… "How was the Universe created?" The ultimate question, and I was pretty chuffed with myself (the ego part of me), because I thought I had stumped the all-knowing. And then, without a second to spare, I receive the words (and I use "receive" because I'm not hearing them, I'm feeling them), "where does a circle begin and end". I was blown away. As if the entire Universe was revealed to me on a silver platter. So I kept asking questions, some cosmic in nature, and others much more personal. And everything was answered, INSTANTLY, without hesitation, with conviction, clear, in a way that not only I can receive but that I can also translate into words I understand. After what felt like 30 minutes of questions, I asked one last question, "This is great, but how can I tap into this when I'm not meditating for 3 hours?", and I received, "remove the veil". I knew exactly what that meant, let me interpret; the veil we have between us and the ether is thin. We can see through the veil to the other side, because the other side is inside, outside, every side, and yet we wear the veil like armour, shielding ourselves from the all-knowing, thinking that it's hard, thinking that we can't possibly know, thinking that it's impossible to know. But just like the Universe as a circle, time and space is also like a circle, it's always now, just move the dial to where you want it to go. When I came back to my conscious state and I was sharing with the group, I blurted out, without consciously thinking about it, "I turned the God Switch on", and from then on, that's always what I've called it. And now whenever I want a revelation instantly, I tap into the part of me that knows that God is me and I make sure the God Switch is on and I ask my questions.

-

Let's talk about drugs that induce spiritual transcendence. I want to preface by telling you where I sit when it comes to these types of drugs. You will only personally experience what you need to for growth and transcendence. Hence why not all experiences work for everyone. Does that discount their ability to take you to places beyond this physical realm? No, of course not. But here's how I see it. Drugs, especially plant medicines, can be used to allow for a portal opening to the spirit world, but when taken, often the experience cannot be controlled. It is like a quick hit of dopamine. Looking for the quick high. And the experience is so life-altering that many get addicted to the experience, calling for the habitual use of plant medicine to relive the experience. However, in my opinion, the better way to open the portal to the spirit world is through meditation. Commitment to a meditation practice, will over time, allow for an almost instant opening of the portal, in which you have complete control over the experience. I like to refer to this experience as "turning the God Switch on". This approach is like serotonin. A slow-release method, but extremely effective. There is longevity in this approach.

-

One of my dear friends has had some trialling times. Physically, emotionally and mentally. And as always, I regularly check in and send him love, my next mode of projected light is to pray for him. This is how I prayed today: Divine Guidance, I pray that he feels the love that he is. I pray that any resistance to well-being dissipates. I pray that strength and enlightenment engulf him. I pray that he remembers the infinity of souls and that the temporary physical journey is designed to teach us love, and when the soul is ready, we will always choose to move on. I pray that he is showered in Golden Light so that his shadows see their own light. I pray that any perceived pain is healed. I pray that he remembers his own Divinity - and that remembering leads to joy, alignment and unconditional love. May peace be upon him. And so it is. Amen.

Why am I sharing this? Because praying for others is the purest form of love possible. When you want blessings for others while expecting nothing in return, when you devote your time with God to benefit another, you express unconditional love, and love with no conditions IS the love of God. We know that there are no others, we know that God is just the part of us that offers no resistance. So when we pray for another to God, we are praying to ourselves for ourselves. There is no deeper love than sincere prayer for self, through the prayer of "others". And when we pray in this way, as we say the words (or more so offer the vibration), the prayer is answered just as quickly as we offer the prayer. As I pray for your healing, you are healed, and as you are healed, so am I in your image.

-

Sometimes the feeling of being safe is so addictive that we get attached to anything that makes us feel safe. That includes, undesired experiences, because it's the devil we know. Some of us are attached to the idea of healing because it is a pain that we know, inadvertently making us feel "safe". So we find things to confirm that we need to be healed, we find things to focus upon that support our true desire, and that is the desire to feel safe, and we find safety in the predictable future (cue Dr Joe Dispenza's voice here). We fixate on the idea that we want a different experience while running on the mouse wheel, taking the same actions, eating the same food, saying the same things. We emit a vibration who's frequency is that of limiting beliefs. We say we want to be free, but we are addicted, and then projecting that addiction of feeling safe, even in the discomfort that we so willingly say we don't want to experience. There is discord. Most of my clients will ask this question, "how am I doing it wrong Gee?". And I say, "you aren't doing it wrong, you are doing it right, you are just focused on the wrong outcome. You say you want to be free, and yet you show up every week telling me how the week revealed to you all the ways in which you aren't free. That tells me that you are focused upon the safety of not feeling free. Your current reality is the sum of the vibration you have been offering." True freedom is to know you are already free. You have to want the discomfort of an unknown comfort more than you want the comfort of a known discomfort. And until that scale is tipped, you will be living a limited life.

-

Praying for salvation. Often when humans get sick or are nearing the end of this physical cycle, I hear people "pray to save them [from death]", as though death weren't a natural part of this experience. Or they pray that the person is healed [from illness or disease]. I often send light to those who need it or request it. But when someone is "dying" (a very human perspective, because we know that we don't die, we instead transition into a different form), I don't pray for their wellness. I pray for their soul to lead the way to the path the soul chose. And I pray that that path is of light, love and alignment. Because once they feel alignment, their resistance to their own well-being will dissipate. And if their soul is ready to transition into a different form, and so it is. I pray that the perceived pain of those around them is softened. I pray that among the perceived physical pain, they feel an innate peace that their soul is leading the way and that all is well and all is as it should be, and that every state is temporary except that of love. No mistakes have been made, no one is getting punished, and there will be no loss. Only a moving breath from this form to another. One that is necessary for our expansion. This doesn't discount the human perspective and experience. We mourn, we feel loss, we feel separation, we empathise, we don't want anyone to feel discord or pain. But beyond the human experience, we are reminded of our Divinity, and with it, our eternalness. Don't pray for me to stay alive, pray that I have lived fully as my soul had intended, and pray that my soul (my higher self) knows the path that serves my highest good, and pray that whatever remaining of this journey, it is filled with love and light, and pray that our love transcends time and space, and knows no bounds, and as my soul transitions from this form to the next, with it, it carries a story (an energetic current) of love that will be forever with me, with you, with us. We are not of limited minds, so we don't need to live in a limited world.

-

Trauma and healing. You will never be the person that existed before the trauma. So you will never heal (although you know my perspective on "healing") and be what was. Instead you will be aware of the discord and move through it to be who you are right now. To stop resisting the well-being that is you in the present moment. And if it wasn't for the trauma, contrast, misguided illusions and perceived pain, you wouldn't be the expanded version of you that you are right now. I never want to be who I was, I want to be who I am now, having moved through the resistance that was preventing me from feeling aligned with who I am right now.

CHAPTER 2

LIBERATION

Free the mind. There are no limitations. We are free. Completely free. The more we understand that we come from love and to love we shall return, the more we understand our unlimited power to create and become anything we desire. We have an untapped power within our thoughts and belief system. If I believe I am something, then I am. I am healed because I am the healer. All ailments can be cured. All disease can disappear. I can change my physical appearance in any way if I believe I can. I wholeheartedly believe in the power of our thoughts. I believe I am who I believe I am - and I'm not just referring to embodiment, I'm referring to physiology. I believe I can change what I will to change, just by changing my belief system. I believe in the power of our thoughts. I believe that we can (re)program ourselves to be who we desire to become.

And thought alone may not hold all the power, but the feelings that the thoughts give me do, because they emit a vibrational frequency that determines what I allow to flow to me, what I attract. If I am experiencing disease, I am in fact experiencing dis-ease, non-alignment with who I truly am. Non-alignment with love and well-being. Dis-ease is just the resistance to ease.

Freedom would look so good on you. One of my favourite mantras is "I am living my best life." Use it as often as you can. When someone asks how you are, respond with the mantra. When you get up to grab a glass of water, say your mantra. Feel the energy of those words. Feel how free you are to live your best life. You are free. You always have been. You always will be. Keep living your best life.

ANDREAS

FROM CANCER TO LIBERATION - A REFLECTION FROM HIS DAUGHTER

November 2011, the world he once knew would never be the same. 46 years old, in-the-night seizure that was just spotted by his wife, a scan and a doctors appointment. All to be told that he had a tumour growing in his brain and with no medical insurance, his best option was to go to emergency immediately. The hospital was called and notified (that didn't prevent the four hour wait - once neurology found out that we were waiting he was seen instantly). The day that followed was a public holiday, so two days later he had surgery for the removal of most of the tumour. Confirmation received that it was in fact cancer. Stage 2 Astrocytoma. Months of recovery, and due to his epileptic seizures, the unlikely chance that driving was in his foreseeable future. Following surgery he wasn't the same. Always a spiritual man, this experience magnified any connection he had to God. For weeks he would only speak of what he saw when he was "on the other side", he spoke in tongues when he slept and would often reference the messages he received from Archangel Gabrielle. (It should be noted at this point that many years before this he had suffered with achalasia which caused him to flatline on the operating table which induced another "spiritually enlightening experience".) I would pray multiple times a day; "bring my dad back, I need him", because as he was now, I couldn't communicate with him on this physical plane. He was in limbo. Stuck between the world of the stars and this physical world. His body was here, but his mind was not. And I wanted him back. Eventually he came back... Many relapses later, so many trials and tribulations, but more than anything a beautiful blooming of love. I was witnessing the greatest story of human (and supernatural) willpower that I had ever come across. We found so much beauty in this journey, so much appreciation for what cancer had taught us about love, and the irrefutable proof that your mind can and literally does change your reality. Not once did my dad complain or feel sorry for himself. He definitely made note of facts - if he was in pain he would follow through with a remedy. But his optimism inspired me. To this day, cancer still in his brain, if you were to ask him how he is, he will respond, "Fantastic!". The struggle was never the physical, I think his Special Forces background made him resilient when it came to physical pain. But the mental struggle... Well that's to be expected. Once a "free man" and now confined and imprisoned in his own home because he was unable to drive or even care for himself at times. Pills upon pills a day changing his chemistry and inducing lethargy, dizziness, ornery feelings... How do you free yourself from that pain...? And again, he inspired me, with his unwillingness to give up. He had always been an artist, but now with a new found subject, it's as though God spoke through him. For all the words he could never say, he drew lines on his canvas. I would watch him work day after day, everyday, many taking months to complete, but always a masterpiece. This came with it's own struggle, he had to nap many times throughout the day, he even suffered a stroke which saw his hand become temporarily immobile - which at the time felt like the end of another source of hope, yet he was immeasurably grateful for what he had created up to that point. I know he's my dad and I'm bias, but I would spend hours exploring each, and for me each one told a story of his struggle, resilience, breakthrough and liberation. And whatever I thought he had suppressed, came through in each of his art pieces. I am in awe of his work and as I continue to explore them, I am honoured that I get to embrace a piece of his life, a piece of his mind and a piece of his story. His work is a reflection of him. And I can't begin to understand what he feels, but his art allows me to understand what I feel about how he expresses what he feels. And isn't that the most poetic story that ever existed. To my dad, and to all of you, with love.

-

Let's talk about fear real quick. Fear feels very real. It can completely change the chemistry of your brain, alter the way your body feels and looks. It can cause an immense feeling of stress and overwhelm. And when you're in it, it can feel that there is no end in sight, and although it is temporary, it feels like it's constant. But here is the truth, the truth that you already know, but the truth that I need to remind you of, fear is not real, once you push past the boundary of the idea of fear you are completely free. Liberated by your inner power to create whatever feeling you desire. Energy and positivity are streams that must flow through your entire life. I cannot say that I am working to be successful in business by thinking my desires into existence using positive thoughts if I wasn't transcending that idea in all facets of my life. I desired to be physically fit, moving my body as often as I could in whichever way felt like the most joyous, I desired to be internally healthy, eating from the earth and thanking my body for taking care of me and loving food the way food loves me, I desired to be mentally healthy, yoga, meditating, praying, giving, being kind, forgiving, releasing, surrendering. I desired that my whole life was to be a stream of positivity. For that to happen I needed to have faith that it would be. I needed to believe that my life was the best it has been and that it could only get better. Whenever fear stepped in my way, I would confront it and did NOT GIVE UP on my desire to live the most incredible life imaginable. Because fear is an illusion, an illusion that I have made real. Because we are the dreamers of our dream, we determine what our canvas looks like, I determine if I am to feel fear or if I am to feel faith. And it's in my knowing that fear is an illusion that I regain my power to move past that fear and into the welcoming arms of faith. The thing that matters most, is this journey, the journey happening right now on your way to your desire. This is what you will remember, the moment before it all happened, because the truth is that it is already happening. In every moment you are being given lessons, winks, high fives, miracles, it's up to you to acknowledge that they exist and EMBRACE them. And you decide whether the journey is filled with fear and contrast or whether it's filled with faith and joy.

-

So during my last trip in Bali (note that when you read this, there may have been many trips in between, but this statement is true as I'm writing this now), my parents were also on vacation in Greece. My dad was born in Thessaloniki, Greece. He moved to Australia when he was 22, to meet my mum. My mum and him were pen pals. A year later, they married. When he came here, he left his whole life behind. His 3 older brothers, his parents, his friends, everything he had ever known growing up. Since building a life in Australia, he lost his dad, flew back for the funeral and then one of his brothers, flew back for the funeral. This was a surprise trip that my mum had organised because my dad wanted to see his two brothers and mum. Since my dad has had cancer, what would be overlooked by the average person, is amplified for my dad. So even the slightest detour of his known course can cause an extreme level of stress, inducing a seizure. Seeing his family, his old friends, his town, where he grew up, was incredibly emotional for him. And one night, when my parents were out with the family, my dad had a really big seizure. He was put into hospital. But Greek hospitals aren't Aussie hospitals. The level of care he received was not comparable to the level of care he is used to here in Australia. My mum was incredibly stressed and worried. When they called me to tell me the news, my first thought was that I had to fly to Greece. My parents were in a foreign country, my sister was alone at home, and I was in Bali, feeling helpless. One night my mum called me hysterical. She was balling her eyes out. I was out for dinner with friends, I immediately screamed, thinking my dad had died. He hadn't. She was just overwhelmed and worried, because of the consistent seizures. He couldn't speak or communicate and his condition was getting progressively worse. I was emotional, and wanted to fly out in the morning. I called my dear friend, who is a fellow coach, and I asked him for his rational mind. He made me realise that there was nothing I could do there, that I couldn't do here. And he was right. I called the insurance company, I consoled my mother, I consoled my sister, and I did what I know to do… Pray. I reached out to ALL my people; my friends, my followers, my light workers, my healers, my readers, my family, everyone. And I asked everyone to pray for him. I gave no one details, only my nearest and dearest knew the specifics. But I asked everyone to pray. Three of us were at my villa, and we held a prayer circle for him. We each journeyed into his body and sent light. One entered his blood, I entered his heart and another danced with him. As I was sending him light and praying I saw his hospital room filled with angels. The angels were everywhere, and I was told that all is well. It was just his body's way of resting. He needed rest. The very next day, was the first day in many days that he could talk (broken speech, but still legible). We FaceTimed and the first thing he said to me was, "I could feel you all praying for me". I cried. He then followed it with, "my room is full of angels, I can see them". I cried some more. As much as we can try to understand, we will never fully understand the force of love that is supporting us, guiding us, holding us in the spirit world. Whatever we imagine, it's more. And when we collectively pray, on this side of the fence (there is no fence, but just for the sake of words), everything is amplified on the other side, legions upon legions of angels, spirit guides, ancestors and God (the collective energy of souls) is answering those prayers. We are loved beyond measure. Imagine that. You cannot ever measure that love, therefore you cannot ever fully understand it. And yet, the proof of that profound love, shows up in uncountable ways, everyday. The magnitude of that, I will never take for granted.

REFLECTION

Rebellion. I try to do at least one rebellious act per day. And rebellious doesn't have to mean outrageous. In order to grow, I like to step outside of my comfort zone, I want to feel uncomfortable, I want to challenge the status quo. I want to do things my way (because I make the rules about my life). I want to honour the crazy ideas that live inside my head. Sometimes I wish people could take tours of my thoughts, so that they could begin to understand me, but then I remind myself that there's no fun in being understood. I am living my best life, are you…?

AFFIRMATION

"I am falling into something different with a new capacity to be beautiful. This transformation is everything I asked for and I will flow with it and not resist it."

We can choose to have a victim mindset or we can choose to have a liberated mindset. I can choose to be a victim of my circumstances and choose to blame everything and everyone else for the way my life is, OR I can choose to take my power back and feel 100% responsible for the way my life is unfolding. Someone once said to me, "you have me to thank for that." And I replied with, "no… I have ME to thank for that." You see, if I give someone else the power over my wins, I would be quick to give someone else the power over my trials. And I'm not about that life. I know that I am inspired, led, guided and even conditioned, but it is me (and God within me) that creates my life. I am responsible for the way it feels, the way it looks, the way it's manifesting. I allow into my experience what I choose to allow, consciously or unconsciously.

-

BALI

Mumma Gaia, mother earth, Divine Feminine, sacred womb, vortex of Source, all that I am. Bali opened me up. Not like a blooming flower, slowly and softly, but more like an exploding star, unraveling, enraging into the Goddess that is me. I am never getting closer, because you can't get closer to that which you already are, instead you can open yourself up to it. See what isn't beyond, but what is within. An island, surrounded by the energetic current of ocean, engulfed in the earth's breath. Just as breath is our life force, the ocean breathes us in and exhales what we aren't. She feeds us her magic by allowing us to flow through her, to live inside her womb. I know what you're thinking right now, Gee, where are you going with this…? I want to share my Bali reflections with you. Because I have chosen to really take it all in here, observing the collective and seeing me through their offerings. As I sit here writing at a beautiful cafe that has amazing Chi energy, surrounded by beautiful high vibe people, and I don't just mean beautiful as in kind, I mean complete embodiment of beauty that they radiate a frequency so in alignment with Source that it has no choice but to change the frequency of the entire room, and as I write these words, and you read them, know that that energy, from the mother, from the father, from me, from them, is transferred to you, planting a seed of love in your heart. Now your only job is just to water that seed.

Here is something that I channeled while in Bali recently:

Our emotions are like flowing rivers, ever changing, constant and unpredictable. There is a harsh brutality that our minds can often inflict upon us, causing pain from the very roots of our thoughts and our choices. Of course all pain is perceived pain, and is an illusion. But when we believe the illusion, the illusion feels real, and therefore we feel the pain as though it were real.

There is always a greater lesson in the shadows. Something deeper than what appears. Just like a river, there is a depth beneath the surface that we cannot see from above. We must go within it to understand it fully.

It won't happen through one session of shadow work, this takes habitual practice.

When I pulled a card for the collective, the Three of Swords came through. This card is about transforming pain and fear into love through shadow work. There is a deep sense of healing and the intention to shift the way you perceive your outer world by observing and even manipulating the way you feel within.

There is a strong focus of transmutation through the heart.

It's always very interesting when I pull cards for the collective, because I notice patterns when I work with my clients, that often the big themes are consistent among all of them. Sitting with your shadows is a beautiful experience. We don't need to be afraid of our shadows, because it's in the darkness that we can birth light.

PRAYER

Divine Guidance, let us see through the eyes of love, let us feel ourselves as we truly are. Let us be receptive to your messages. Let our intuitive nudges be so clear and so vivid that we never be able to mistake them. Guide us on our path so that we shall never get it wrong. Bring to us what is rightfully ours, as we were already born into this world with them. Thank you for all that I am, all that I have and all that I am becoming. I love you. And so it is. Amen.

-

So someone recently asked me why the Law of Attraction didn't work for everyone. This is how I responded; All the laws of the universe are ALWAYS working. Gravity doesn't just work for some of us, it works for everyone, always. The Law of Attraction is ALWAYS working. If the results aren't desirable, it's because the vibration being offered isn't in alignment with the desire. All you need to do is match the frequency. Some do that with visualisation and other "manifesting" tools and some just wake up, say thank you and smile at strangers everyday. There are no rules as to how you use the law (which is always in motion) in your favour. When you know this, you can choose to be more intentional with the vibration you're offering. You will receive in return what you emit. Period.

-

One of my favourite spiritual tools is the use of visualisation. To visualise is to bring a future projection into the present moment and to make it real now. Just as described in Chapter 7, time is not linear. And I can make all things desired real in the present moment, just as I can make all my memories real in the present moment, and I do this by evoking the feelings of the experience/thing/person now. When you think of your last birthday, you can recall what you ate, what you wore, who you were with, who called, maybe even who didn't, the gifts you received, and the memory of those moments evoke emotions in the present moment. You are altering your body chemistry just by thinking a thought. So why wouldn't we do that for our "futures" too? There are many ways to visualise, you can use the creative visualisation practice, where you sit in a comfortable position and for anywhere between 1-5 minutes you create a scenario in your mind of something that you want to experience. And you play it like a real-time movie, adding in all the details, feeling all the feelings, using all your senses to make the experience feel real. And each time you can play a new scene. So for example, if my desire is to travel to luxurious places all over the world, each time I use creative visualisation, I would picture a different location, different modes of transport, different cultural experiences. But the theme remains the same. Another useful way to use visualisation is through meditation. For 6 months I religiously listened to Dr Joe Dispenza's Guided Space Meditation. After around 40 mins, he takes you on a visualisation quest, where you begin to imagine your ideal life (or at least an element of it), as you are already in a deep meditation (close to a hypnotic state), you are offering no resistance to the desired experience, making it feel incredibly real and offering the vibration of it, bringing about the physical realisation of it faster, collapsing time and space. Another way to visualise is through the use of Vision Boards or Vision Statements (both which I've described in this book). There are many ways to visualise, find a way that feels good to you and use it as a tool to come to the realisation of all that is already so faster.

People often ask me what I "do", and I reflect on this question, because it's less about what I do and more about who I "be". But the most common answer I give is that I am a Mindset Coach that helps people reprogram their subconscious minds so that they can more closely expand with the Universe and remember who they are; love. Of course the next question is always, "how do you do that?". And to put it simply it is this; your subconscious mind, and the beliefs that come from the neural pathways in your subconscious mind, are there because of habitual thoughts and behaviours. Often learned patterns. So to rewire your brain and to reprogram your subconscious mind, we need to create new habitual thoughts and patterns. So the work we do together is understanding, with clarity, what you want, and then how to create beliefs that support what you want. And then, most importantly how to create those belief systems so that they feel real in your mind, so that you will act on those new beliefs. This part varies for everyone. Personally, I am a very visual person, so drawing, Vision Boards, Vision Statements, Journaling, are all very effective for me. Whereas others prefer mantras, affirmations, support groups, positivity apps, podcasts, hypnotherapy, meditation, etc. The "how" is subjective, highly personal. So what works for others, may not work for you. The commonality is that it requires habitual work. Your willingness to evolve needs to match your desire to evolve. There is no quick fix, you don't go to the gym one time and suddenly have a six pack. You need to consistently take habitual action and over time, that habitual behaviour becomes learned and you do it on auto-pilot. I wake up and go to the gym every morning because it is just what I do now, and I know that that habit aligns with the person I want to be. And so I am. Does that make sense? If you want that, then you need to *be* that first in order to realise that you are already that.

-

DECLARATION

The portal to self. The doors have opened, I have decided, I reap the rewards and savour the fruit of the seeds I planted, nurtured and sowed. As the wild card appears, the infinite possibilities are realised. The planets have aligned. The timing is right. The Universe said YES! I have the Midas Touch. Great leaps have been made. Great distances have been traveled in a short space of time. I am swimming with the cosmic current of life - and it feels so fucking good. I am grateful. I have finally realised all that I have desired, and it feels so aligned, as though it were always here, but now I am tuned into the physical frequency of it. I feel free. I feel aligned with my well-being. I am flowing with the Universal current of abundance - the ever-abundant Universe that I am. I have opened my heart to expansive love. Feeling it now, I am reminded of all the lifetimes before where I lived this truth. I feel incredibly blessed. Thank you Big G. The timing is right. I love you. Amen.

CHAPTER 3

TO KNOW SELF IS TO KNOW GOD

My only true desire. *"The desire to know your own soul will end all other desires."* - Rumi. The better I know myself, the better I know everyone, the better I know God.

The search is always from within. If you feel you have more to discover, spend more time with yourself. You will discover a whole new world. A whole new potential. A whole new peace. Most of my self-love practices involve a deep focus on transformation and awareness. Designed to ease you into a pattern of self-awareness. It won't be like a flood, as idealistic as that may be to imagine, it'll be like small waves washing onto the shore. Embrace the small steps, because they are in fact giant leaps.

Our ego tries to complicate things. But our spirit is simple. When you find yourself over analysing - come back to your true self and watch how easily the anxious feelings dissolve.

To be yourself… This is so easy to say and for a lot of us, harder to implement. But you need to know that it is in fact easy, it's easy because it's our natural way of being. To be yourself, you just have to do what your soul is telling you to do. Even if it doesn't make sense, follow your soul. And I have to be honest with you, I don't always listen to my soul. Sometimes I shut it out and try to use my "logic" and it almost never pays off when it's not aligned with my soul. But it's time, it's time to honour your soul and love yourself.

Follow your soul, it knows the way. Just take some time to do absolutely nothing and just rest your mind. Things will begin to appear in your mind. You will feel a deep sense of pulling towards something. Listen. Follow through. It's all there for you.

Atticus once said, don't believe the lies that you are not who you can be. Everything I believe is true - so I need to make sure that my mind isn't filled with lies.

The idea of God has always been a reflection of us. When being male, superior, dominant, dictatorial was the common belief - that's the image of God we created. Our idealistic reflection. When being open, infinite, loving and always present was the common belief - that's the image of God we created. Again, our idealistic reflection. I am not God, but God is me. God is the reflection of the collective consciousness. And so a shift in the collective truth lies in a collective movement, a shift of perception of what it means to see through the eyes of God. To know self is to know God. The collective consciousness shift begins within you alone. The deeper you know yourself, the deeper your love and acceptance of self, the richer the love of the collective. The love and nurturing you give to yourself, is the love and nurturing that you give to the entire planet.

You are not here to learn, you are here to remember. It seems familiar because it is. You give life to your thoughts. And those thoughts, sometimes conditions from this world, but sometimes ideas from other worlds, that you have brought with you here. That can mean whatever you desire it to mean. In fact, I am certain that your perception of it will be a reflection of who you are in this moment. Regardless of your emotional reaction, the answer lies within. How do you feel right now? How can you choose to feel better right now? Can you choose to live right now?

This is a train of thought, this is how your mind works. It is not linear, you think through your connections to a previous thought. Your current thought leads to the next thought and so on. And we can allow our thoughts to control us, or we can be conscious and intentional with our thoughts and program our minds to lead us to the life we desire. What do you want to experience? What thoughts, beliefs and feelings will lead to that experience?

GOD IS ME

PRAYER

And so it is God, and so it is. Let me come to the physical realisation of (insert desire), which already exists within me vibrationally. My life is perfect and I am so grateful for all that I have and all that I am - that is, EVERYTHING. And I know that although you live within me, YOU know what's best for me, and I trust the Divine timing of my life and I know that it is always dependent on my alignment (with you) - my relationship with myself, and I ask that you guide me - light up the path, so that I can feel it so vividly within me that I won't question it, because it will feel like an extension of myself. I love you, and my gratitude for your love for me can never be truly expressed through words, but my love for me, is a true representation of my gratitude for your love Big G. Divinely connected and infinite love. Amen.

Be playful with God. God never intended for His glory to get misconstrued and idolised. He wants you to know that He lives within you, and that the more fun you have, the better you'll feel, and thus, the better God feels, and the more you both (but really one and the same) expand and become more of yourself.

(For reference, I refer to God as "He" and the Universe as "She" just to make it easier to transcribe my reflections, not that I in any way believe that source energy has a specific gender identity.)

-

You are always one with the Universe. And thus one with everything and everyone. But there will be times where the conditions and environments around us make us feel out of touch with this truth. But it only takes one conscious and intentional decision to come back to the feeling place of oneness. Just decide that it begins now.

Imagine you have a box in your lap and within it there are a thousand small blocks, each with a word; "condition", "doubt", "fear", "comparison", "limit", "condition", "worry", "anxiety", "expectation", "condition". In your hands you have blocks with the words, "love", "peace", "oneness", "abundance", "joy", but you haven't made room in your box for them. And so you continue to experience the same pattern of habitual thoughts, beliefs, feelings and actions because you haven't allowed the space for your new blocks to plant themselves.

In our minds, there is infinite space. But we tend to focus more on our unwanted feelings and experiences - wishing they were different. Watering the seeds of the trees we do not wish to grow.

-

How you reprogram your subconscious thoughts...

Take any area of your life where you offer resistance. And by resistance, I'm alluding to resistant thoughts that prevent you from feeling your innate alignment with the Divine (and all Divine things, feelings and experiences). Write a list. This list is for you, so don't hold back, don't lie to yourself, don't shy away from a thought just because you don't want it to be a dominant thought. Write it all down. Whatever wants to come through.

Once revealed, ask two questions for each thought, "Is this thought serving me?" and "Does this thought make me feel good?".

The answer to both questions should be YES. And if the answer isn't yes, then the thought needs to change.

When I work with clients, when we get to this point, we have options; it may be as simple as verbalising the truth (your truth) and questioning whether the thought aligns with that truth, and if it doesn't replacing it with a thought that does. This is called "flipping the switch" and is highly effective for most misguided beliefs. But sometimes we have deep programmed conditioned beliefs that have come from our childhood or specific experiences that require deeper work. We need to figure out where the thought came from, how the thought has served us up until now (usually keeping us safe in some way and also allowing us to plant seeds of desire because of the experience of contrast that the thought fixated on) and then reconstruct our truth so that we can then change the belief. Because if your "truth" aligns with the misguided belief, then it's the truth that needs to change and not the belief. Our collection of beliefs become our truth. So the beliefs depend on the truth, but the truth only exists because of our beliefs. The paradox of the subconscious. You are what you repeatedly think about, you've heard that before right?! But what you think about is often dependent on what you've always habitually thought about. So to break free you must intentionally plant the seeds of new thoughts and consciously make an effort to bring those new thoughts to your awareness as often as possible so that they become your dominant thoughts, therefore reprogramming your subconscious mind. And as those thoughts begin to change, and with them your beliefs and your ultimate truth, then so does your physical reality. It begins to match the truth that has become you. The formula, although relatively simple in theory, in practice can prove a little more difficult. Because when you're so used to thinking a thought, and you have other thoughts that support that thought, if we want to get science involved, you have to create new neural pathways in your brain so that your thought patterns can change. This is the work. It won't be easy, and yet it really is easy. Make it a habit to think the new thought(s) and through repetition, you will create the new neural pathways.

-

I read today, "Be grateful for triggers, they point where you are not free". And it inspired a train of thought for me. Contrast, which can sometimes look like pain, is there to serve us. Sometimes it allows us to clarify what we do want to experience, sometimes it reveals the parts of us that we need to heal (and by heal, I mean shift perception), sometimes it directs us, sometimes it opens us up to growth and sometimes it is the moment before a breakthrough. But in whichever way it shows up, it is always there to serve us. Because it leads us to self-reflection, to asking questions, like "why", and those questions give us choices (free-will), to either be dependent on knowing the answer or surrendering because the higher part of us already knows and is guiding us.

Beliefs are conditional. They limit us, because as soon as we believe something, our entire perception of this 3 Dimensional world is conditioned by that belief. Because the belief itself is powerless, but as soon as I act (and act, can be physical or mental in this context) on that belief, I bring it to life.

When I work with clients on belief patterns and The Laws of the Universe, I often hear people say, "I believe X, but…" and as soon as they add the word "but", I know that what they really believe is what follows and not what preceded. This is conscious active mind versus subconscious mind. You can consciously say that you believe X, "but" your conditioned subconscious beliefs are what control your perception and interpretation of your reality. And your beliefs are your truth. And whether that truth is valid or not, when you get out into the world, you will project your truth out onto the world, and also perceive from that level of understanding. So your reality becomes distorted, because it is attached to your beliefs, and often beliefs haven't come from your interpretation of the Universe's messages, but instead from the conditioning that society has projected onto you since you were born. It is intentional systematic programming. But now you know. Therefore you now have the power to shift your perception and reprogram your beliefs. So that they are no longer beliefs, but instead energetic truth. My belief system is based on how an idea makes me feel. If it feels good, then it's in alignment with my soul, therefore in alignment with God. If it doesn't feel good, then it mustn't be truth, therefore it shouldn't be a dominant thought in my mind.

You have complete control over your alignment with that which you want. You are aligning yourself energetically, and once you fully believe that you are a vibrational match, and so it is. As soon as you ask, you receive, the time delay is always about how long it takes you to become a vibrational match so that you can finally come to the realisation of what is. Consider it done. Done in your mind, done in your body, done in your soul. You are there.

Every time you make a choice in your mind, you are actually making a Quantum Jump. The Quantum Field is best understood like this; look at a door in the room you're in. If I asked you to go to that door, what would you have to do? You would have to get up, take time and space, to walk/run/ dance (etc.) to get yourself to that door. Ok, now, if I ask you to close your eyes and imagine that you're already in front of that door, could you do it? Of course you can. That's the Quantum Field, where time and space is non dominant and reality is flexible, think of it like a pipe cleaner, I can condense or expand time and space. You can be there now, just by allowing from the Quantum Field.

-

Let's talk about beliefs real quick. Beliefs in themselves are a source of confinement. To have a belief that I am unwilling to allow evolve, suggests that I am confined to a predetermined life. My beliefs today, allow me to project my truth in this way, but I am very open to my beliefs evolving as I learn, channel and experience new (or I should say, "remembered", as in coming from the collective consciousness) things. The fluidity of beliefs keep us free, allowing us to hold our power.

-

I recently read something on Ezer Magazine that became a catalyst for a train of thought that I wanted to share with you. What I read was this; "Part of our problem is that all too often we assume that God is not meeting our needs or is holding back in some way. When, in reality, He is meeting our needs in His capacity - an all-knowing one - instead of ours - a limited one." Your perspective will always be limited because there will always be things the physical part of us does not know (or realise). It's impossible to be all-knowing as physical beings. The spirit (as in the spiritual part of us) is all knowing but we (as in the physical part of us) would not function if we were all knowing. It would be too much information. So our perspective will always be limited. But God, as in the part of you that IS all knowing, is ALL knowing. And you can always trust that perspective. So what I'm saying is that, yes God is all knowing, and God is you, therefore you are of the all-knowing. But you, as in the physical part of you, the part of you with a conscious mind, is limited, because we cannot realise our all-knowingness as physical beings.

-

Let's talk about our identities for a minute. We spend so much time trying to figure out who we are, we attach ourselves to a fixed identity, as though it could be defined in a sentence. We spend a lifetime trying to become one perfect person, forgetting all the while that we are never just one person. In fact, in this lifetime alone you have been thousands of people. You were a baby, you were a toddler, you were a child, you were a teenager, you were a young adult, you were an adult, you were a mother, you were a father, you were a friend, you were a lover, you were a dancer, you were a chef, you were a nurse, you were all of these things. We are designed to be ever-evolving. Never the same person for more than a moment. The moment that exists now, is a moment more than existed before. And how can my identity from the moment before embody who I am now, when I will always be more than I was before. Fixed identities are flawed, because they discount our ever-evolving nature. Expansion cannot be given an identity, and we are here to expand, sometimes even ferociously. So if you have been searching for who you are, search no more, for you are already of the defined, and that is love. But how that love evolves requires no identity, because that ever-expanding love will always be more than it was before, it will always be everything, and it will always be something that words will never be able to truly define. To define in this instance, would be to confine, to limit, to reject the all-embodying nature of you.

-

Is this information profound? It may be. But it doesn't need to be. Is all of this probably already out there in the ether? Of course it is, can we say that any information is unique when it comes from the collective consciousness anyway. Is there ever an original thought? Or are each of us just trying to interpret the all-knowing into words that maybe someone else will understand? That's what I'm trying to do here. You don't need to read any of this and think that one piece of it will profoundly change your life, but collectively, as you read these words, many that you may have heard before, you will begin to consciously reprogram your subconscious mind, because now the ideas that you may have heard before are being delivered in a new way, and maybe, just maybe, this time they will be understood differently, in a way that you can apply them. You are here reading this now for a reason, and there is something here for you. You don't need to look for the reason, it will appear to you. As if by magic, it will reveal itself. And although the words may not be profound, your understanding of them will be. And that profoundness will be completely unique to you, because your perception IS your reality. How you read this book, or more so, how you understand this book will be dependent on your personal perception (that comes from your experience, your brain, your thoughts, your everything), and then that personal perception will apply the profound understanding in a way that is serving to your life. It will all fall into place perfectly, in the most Divine way and time. And in my pursuit to channel a book filled original thought, I'm reminded that there is no original thought, instead it is just my interpretation of the ultimate truth, translated to you in a way that it can be received. God works through us, and he doesn't choose one person over another, but He does choose the best possible channel. If you are denying yourself of your intuitive gifts, God will find another channel. You don't ever stop having the gift of intuition, but resisting it will mean that you don't get to hear the Universe talk to you. Let me be clear, the Universe is ALWAYS talking to you, but you won't hear it, and if you won't allow yourself to hear it, you can't even attempt to translate it so that it's serving. If I denied myself of the opportunity to translate everything that was coming through me, then this book would never have been written. And I could never possibly measure the impact that this book will have, because as it shifts and awakens one person, that person's awakening may shift and awaken 10 others. So I would be denying the world the possibility to expand in this way, through me as a channel, through you as a channel, and through us all as individualisations of God.

I want to address the original thought concept for a moment longer. I feel that for anyone who questions their own Divinity, is reminded in this moment, that if there are no original thoughts, as everything comes from the collective consciousness, then every thought you think is Divine. Even the thoughts that come from misguided beliefs (from the ego), there is Divinity within them too. Because the ego isn't separate from the collective consciousness, the ego exists within it. It all serves but one purpose, to expand what it is. And the ego acts as a catalyst for contrast which births desire, which allows us to consciously (and unconsciously) expand.

-

Every Wednesday at 11am I jump on a call with two of my friends. We chat for around 30 minutes on anything and everything. Usually esoteric in nature, and although we more than often share information we already know, it has been brought to our conscious awareness in that very moment for a reason (we all know my belief on Divinity)! Today the train of thought between us evolved into the idea of limited consciousness (a very Eckhart Tolle approach to life). We are consciousness (aka God), understanding itself. The best way for consciousness to understand itself is to come into the physical experience with access to limited subjective consciousness, so that it can consciously expand, using the conscious yet limited subjective mind and thoughts. It seems like an interesting concept, that the all-knowing, would want a limited and subjective understanding of itself, and yet it is the only way for it to *truly* understand and know itself. And for those who may not understand what subjective consciousness is, it is the knowing that you are aware of self. You are aware that you are not your thoughts, you are the observer of them. You are the consciousness behind the thought. But the consciousness that you are isn't fully understood, and yet it is who you are. Then comes the idea that, of that subjective consciousness, where the ethereal part of us is interpreting and understanding the physical experience, which of it comes from an intuitive place and which is free will? It's a combination of both. When we listen, we are guided by our intuition, but even with the intuitive nudges, we always have the free will to make a conscious choice, that may reject the intuitive guidance. But just like a navigation system, your free will will not cause you to go off course. You will always be redirected. You can never get it wrong. But the intuitive path will always be faster.

-

Are you cultivating an environment that is conducive for expansion? Or are you denying yourself the opportunity to expand in an easy and effortless way? Easy and effortless in this context, doesn't mean without contrast. The contrast is the precursor for expansion. It is necessary so that we can expand in a conscious way. Because without the contrast, we can't determine what we want to experience. Cultivating an environment that is conducive for expansion is all-inclusive; what do you eat, who are you surrounded by, how do you serve, how often do you laugh, how often do you self-reflect and re-adjust (we don't just want to observe ourselves, we want to shift if necessary for expansion), how do you move and honour your vessel, how do you communicate, how do you love, how deeply do you love. Life will serve you what you serve yourself. Honour thy self, and that self-honouring will attract experiences that honour you. All of this sounds beautiful in theory, but the practical side to this spiritual-knowing isn't always smooth sailing. We get caught up in the matrix. We get busy doing the everyday tasks that require our upkeep. We get drawn into the vortex of routine, we work on auto-pilot. And that's why being self-aware is one of my top two virtues. Self-awareness allows you to observe yourself and determine how far or how close you are to alignment. Once aware, you can move closer to alignment. Closer to cultivating an environment that is conducive for expansion. But self-awareness takes discipline. How often are you willing to commit to self-reflection? How often are you willing to observe yourself, observe your thoughts, your feelings, your behaviour, your friends, your posts, your internal stories, everything that is you...? And then use the information obtained from that observation to shift? The willingness to take action has to match the desire for expansion. Without the willingness to take action, we still maintain the desire, but we separate ourselves from it, it will always be over there, in a place that I may some day get to, but for now I observe it from afar. When the truth tells us that it is always here, I just need to come to the realisation of it. Also note that I reference SELF-awareness and SELF-reflection, because what others are doing, thinking, feeling has no bearing on whether you are cultivating an environment conducive for expansion. Do not give your power away. It is and always will be your perception of reality that IS reality.

-

There are many teachings that exist today. Astrology, numerology, human design, tarot, and so many others that I have been exposed to over my lifetime, and I assume many that I haven't also. And each serve as an expression of the interpreted truth that has been channelled by humans to better understand the Source that we came from and to serve in our purpose, which is our expansion. There is no one teaching that is more right than another. They each offer layers of the ultimate truth. And even within the teachings, there are many interpretations of the channelled information, each providing a different view point. And across the teachings there are similarities and there are differences. Again, none being more right than another. Instead, they are tools, and whichever resonate with you, can become your truth, your tool, your studied craft, your means for deeper understanding and interpretation. But one thing that I know for certain, is that however serving all these tools and teachings are, none are necessary for a full life, one where you will carry out your purpose completely. You will expand, with or without the knowledge. The knowledge will alter and amplify the experience, offering another layer, a depth that serves the collective consciousness. But you will ALWAYS expand, it is our design. So don't buy into the dogmatic approach of these teachings. That your astrology chart will determine your whole life, or your human design is an excuse for the way you are with decision making or people. These tools and teachings allow you to understand your human experience better, but you will always be more spirit. You will always be a spirit (of the collective) having a temporary human experience, designed to expand, to serve the collective Source you came from. So although useful in understanding, don't get caught up in it. Don't let it dictate your decision making, don't let it deter you, don't let it control you. Free will, will always reign. Understanding serves us, because it makes us self-aware on areas where we may be more sensitive than others, but even without the understanding you will be just fine. Don't panic. All is well.

This in no way discounts the validity and impact that these teachings have. I follow and immerse myself in many of these teachings. But over my time coaching, many of my clients find themselves fixated on the details, and I always assure them, that what they're meant to know, they already do, what they're meant to understand, they will. Your intuition is your greatest asset. Greater than any teaching provided on earth. Provided that you know when it is your intuition guiding you.

CHAPTER 4

LOVE IS LOVE IS LOVE IS LOVE

Rumi once said that both light and shadow are the dance of love. I believe that everything is either an act of love or a call for love and the only thing that would make it otherwise is your perception of it. Life, people, the world and everything in between, can be seen through loving eyes. I still love everyone I have ever loved. Love is love is love is love is love is love is love is love is love. Love is infinite. Love is limitless. Love is all encompassing. Love is me. Love is you. Love is God. Love is life. Love is love is love is love is love is love is love.

"Your self love is a medicine for the earth." - Yung Pueblo. We help the world by helping ourselves. Don't mistake this as an excuse to be ignorant to the injustices that happen in the world (we will talk about spiritual bypassing later). But know that your first and foremost job is to love yourself fully and completely and once you begin to overflow with love, let

that love spill out into the world. Stand for love. Stand for self-love. Stand for world love. Love isn't part of the journey. Love is the journey.

What does it mean to be love? To come from love? To be on our journey home to love? To be an expression of love? It is to be in complete harmony with the song of the Universe, to feel the vibration of the Universe pulsing through your body, to embody joy, well-being, freedom, flow.

"You're unhappy because you are not in alignment with who you are. Not because of what anyone else is doing."
-Maryam Hasnaa

Once we take away the blame from others and we focus exclusively internally for the way we feel, we regain our power. Nothing outside of us can control how we feel. We react to the way others treat us because we are not in alignment with who we really are. Once we learn to truly, deeply, intimately love ourselves, we will cease to react at all and we would never want to hurt another human being (or any being) ever again. I often suggest that you look within but many don't really know how to start. A great way to do this initially is to ask yourself, "if money/time/resources weren't an issue, what would I want to do in this moment?"... Then go and do that in any way you can right now. Start to listen to where you're being called. Start to listen to your inner self. Take a step back from the hustle bustle and God will give you all the prompts to move in the direction of your true calling. You are all that you need. Alignment is the new hustle. My life has changed so much since I made this realisation.

FOULA

My mum. The earth angel. The Goddess. The most pure light I have ever felt in my entire life. I honestly have tried to comprehend how my soul was lucky enough to choose her as a mother. I often read stories of people with broken and painful relationships with their parents, and I try to empathise and also acknowledge that it is part of their soul's journey here to learn certain lessons, but the truth for me is that my experience with my parents has been so full. I feel so blessed every single day to have incredible parents who support me in every way. My mum is actually the one who introduced me to the woo woo life. She always had every Law of Attraction book, every inspirational recording and attended so many seminars and talks. And I grew up always rolling my eyes, thinking "what is she up to this time". I was convinced that she lived in a fairy land where all the ideas seemed beautiful and uplifting, but that's where their power ended, none of them would ever amount to results. And it wasn't until I began my own spiritual awakening that I realised how lucky I had been my whole life to have access to so much content and so many spiritual teachers. My mum would play recordings in the car, she would expose me to affirmations and visualisations. She even had so many meditative tracks on CD. And all that aside, my mum is a Saint. I'm officially calling it. Her heart is so pure and so welcoming. I always believed that I was sent to protect her, because she has always been so kind to everyone, and I always worried that she was getting hurt. But she taught me about unconditional love. Everyday she tells me how proud she is of me, how much I inspire her, how much she loves sharing my message, how well I'm doing. She never asked me, "are you making money?", "when are you moving out?", "when are you getting married?", "how many clients do you have?", because to her my measure of success was by how happy I was. And that taught me to measure my success that way too. My mum is the most successful person I know; she loves her job. She is the best beauty therapist in the world. She is excited to work everyday, she puts so much love and heart into her work and people flock to her. She doesn't advertise or have any fancy marketing strategies, she just shows up, expresses her soul purpose and that brings in all the clients she'd ever want. My mum also has an incredible gift for being able to sell absolutely ANYTHING. She has sold artwork, jewellery, so many MLMs (that's a story for another time), her own skincare range (yes, she did that too - one of her lifelong dreams), just to name a few. People buy from her because they trust her, and they trust her because she's authentic. She doesn't pretend to be someone she's not, she shows up as herself, vulnerabilities, insecurities and all, and she let's people in. This is something I'm still learning. I sometimes envy her ability to let people in the way she does, I haven't been able to master that yet, but I'm working on it. She's so willing to help people and SERVE. She taught me service, she taught me love, she taught me forgiveness, she taught me expansion. No one is perfect (although I think she comes close), and sometimes she's not in alignment, and that's where I step in… I can now realign her really quickly, and when I do, I can assure you that my mum will manifest anything she wants VERY QUICKLY. New clients, money, opportunities, people, experiences, anything. Love is drawn to her, because that is her reflection. I recently had a moment where I snapped at her, and my mum gave me space, and as soon as she walked away, I brought myself back into love, and reflected on how my mum has never asked me for an apology, she has always just loved me unconditionally, just as I am, and never required that love to have conditions fulfilled, and that has taught me how to love unconditionally, and to forgive the way God forgives - to know no wrong was done to you. I cry sometimes because I feel so blessed to know her. She's the type of person that if someone spoke bad of her, you just wouldn't believe it. She is love. And I am filled with appreciation that I was able to experience her as my mum. I love you mumma.

-

A reflection on the unpredictability of surrender: this was a post I wrote on Facebook during my time in Bali

So this week was meant to be one of those "Big Launch" weeks. But as you know, when the Universe wants to take you on a journey, most of the time, you have no choice but to ride the wave. Actually riding the wave is best case scenario, my scenario was more like, trying not to drown.

Ready for a story…?

So for those of you unaware, I'm currently living it up in beautiful Bali. Her magic is profound, everything about this place is beyond what is explainable in human language. You come here, and you just know, you feel it. It's an energy that once it moves through you, it never leaves you. But it's also an energy that shakes you up, and it'll either spit you out, or you'll find your feet and be covered in cuts and bruises (yes, literal cuts and bruises).

While I'm in Bali, my parents took a vacay to Greece. Their
motherland. For my dad, it has been an incredibly emotional
experience. Seeing his family again, all the people he grew
up with, his childhood neighbourhood. It has been
overwhelming. And for those of you unaware (many
revelations in this story), my dad has an Astrocytoma (aka. a
form of brain cancer), and that causes him to have seizures
whenever he is stressed, overwhelmed, emotional or
triggered. As relaxed as he has tried to be on this holiday, all
the factors considered, it has all been a little much for him. I
get a call from my mum 5 days ago… My dad is in hospital
having suffered some seizures. Usually, this would be fine,
Melbourne has some of the best neurosurgeons in the world.
Our healthcare system is first class and he is always treated
like royalty. Greece… well not so first class. He was tied up
like a prisoner (added to his stress), the nurses aren't
checking on him at all, and my mum has been emotionally
exhausted being a nurse, a wife, a supporter, a mother, a
foreigner, a tourist, and everything else in between. So can
you imagine, as the rock of the family, the guilt I carried with
me after hearing all this…? I was ready to jump on a plane to
Greece.

I call my friend, and ask him, "am I being emotional, or is this
an intuitive decision?" We both determined that I was in fact

81

being emotional, or at least taking on the emotions of my parents.

I did what I know, that energy is not limited by time and space, and what I could do by being in that room as my physical self, I can also do as my spiritual self from here. And so I prayed, sent light and invited all my lightworker friends to also pray and send light. As I was sending light, I entered my dad's heart, and saw all the angels in his room. I also understood that his soul just needed this time to rest.

Two days later I spoke to him, finally, he was able to communicate with me and he said, "I felt all your prayers, the power of prayer is everything, and my room is filled with angels".

And I wish I could say that that is the end of this story, but it isn't…

For the last four days I have had severe nausea. It's not common for me, in fact I don't ever remember having nausea that lasted more than a few minutes. The only time I've ever experienced severe nausea was when I was on Malaria tablets (a story for another time). But this nausea has been debilitating. Yesterday I spent the entire day in bed. I couldn't move, I wasn't able to drive anywhere (due to dizziness) and my entire body felt like it was dying.

This morning I ordered an IV drip filled with vitamins, saline and a whole bunch of other immunity boosters, to try and replenish. It filled me at first, and it felt great for a few minutes, and then I crashed again. I feel depleted. And those who know me well, know that I am so careful with my spoken word, I don't like to make absolute statements that aren't serving. But right now, I need to honour the fact that my soul is using my body to teach me. Teach me replenishment, teach me rest, teach me to retreat, teach me to honour, teach me how easily I absorb the energy around me.

During this time, I have really missed my family.
I miss my parents, who forever send me love and pray for me.
I miss my sister, who I know would be laying next to me while I replenish, who would bring me snacks to make sure I'm eating (specifically Savoys - they are my "Gee needs comfort food and energy" snack).
I miss my grandma who would have made me hot soup with all my favourite things.

All is well, and I am listening. I am riding the wave and even during the ebb, I am savouring every moment and showing immense gratitude for the ways in which my path is being revealed to me. It's all Divine and I see God in everything, everyone and every moment.

So big launch weeks, productivity and everything else I could have possibly planned, will always come secondary to alignment, self-care and honouring the present moment.

Right now, above all, I am focused on loving myself and my vessel. All else will follow.

I love you.

And thank you to everyone who has been sending me and my family light. I have felt it all.

-

It hasn't fallen into my lap, I have been preparing for this for lifetimes upon lifetimes. I was once doing a past life regression on myself, and as I journeyed through my past lives, whichever were being brought to my awareness, I asked some leading questions about how the visions were to serve me in my current lifetime. And one resounding message was delivered… the conscious part of me felt as though I was consciously manifesting (i.e. coming to the realisation of) things in my present lifetime through my focus upon them now, but in actual fact, so many things were coming to fruition because I had been preparing for them for lifetimes upon lifetimes. And too, there will be things that bare their fruit in lifetimes to come because of things, ideas and seeds that we are planting in this lifetime. The part of us that desires instant gratification, doesn't like to hear this - that is the ego resisting this truth. But the soul, thrives on knowing that it is ever-expanding, and the blessings that are revealing themselves to me now, may have come from many lifetimes ago. The unfolding of this truth led me to another truth and that is that it is not important to know where the realisation has come from. Instead my work is to continue projecting love, continue being love, and that being is what reveals miracles. Love because that is what you are, do not love to gain. Love as though there could be no other way for you to be. And that pure nature is what will bare fruits. There are no accidents, the Divine interweb is perfectly orchestrated. This also explains our free will. Although we have free will in this lifetime, some of our free will was executed in past lives and in the spirit world, which then becomes a soul contract in this lifetime. That's why some things feel like destiny; as in it's pre-determined. Your soul chose to experience it. You can resist these contracts and fight them, but as they are often binding, you will come back again to experience them in another lifetime if you don't live out the debt owed in this lifetime.

PRAYER

Divine Guidance, allow the revelations to be for my highest good and for the highest good of everyone involved. Please allow me to hear, see and feel the Divine Messages that come from my higher self so that I can fully trust and accept the intuitive nudges that come through and then act with conviction from those nudges. Please, whenever I waver, make it easy for me to come back to my Divinity. Today I choose to see and feel my own light, embodying the highest frequency of that which I am. I love you. And so it is. Amen.

-

LOVE IS LOVE IS LOVE IS LOVE

So when I am calling in new clients to work with me, I usually utilise two methods to do this. One, is the use of a sigil. A sigil is an object that you cast an intention into, and then that object represents the intention, so you can then release it and allow the Universe to work her magic. I often use crystals to represent desired clients. I also pray for them. So recently I was calling in three new 1:1 clients. I used clear quartz as sigils. I laid them out at my alter, and gave them a special home. And then I prayed for them;

Divine Guidance, I pray for my three clients. I pray that their perceived pains dissipate, I pray that they realise who they truly are, I pray that the love that engulfs them is so overwhelmingly powerful, that it changes the atmosphere and the course of their lives forever. I pray that they feel held, supported and safe. I pray that their faith is unwavering. I pray that they emit only the highest of frequencies and attract and allow all that they desire. I pray that they remember that they are everything, and to be, do and have it all, all they have to do is realise that they already do. I pray that they remember that they are of God, and that God is love, God is all, therefore they are love, they are all. I pray that they feel this prayer energetically and it shifts something for them. I pray that they feel my love for them. I pray that they know I hold space for them. I'm thankful to see

them, to know them, to be them. And so it is. I love you.
Amen.

The sigils and prayers ALWAYS work. Because it is of love.
And I don't create conditions. There is no time limit and no
"right" way for it to be made manifest. I allow God to move
the energetic call through the right people in Divine timing.
And I pray for them from the deepest parts of my heart,
because as I pray for them, I pray for everyone, I pray for
myself.

-

PRAYER

Divine Guidance, I pray that you lead the way. And as you offer no resistance, allow me to tap into that unrestricted supply. You have all the answers, allow the revelations to flow to me and through me easily and effortlessly. Let my vision for love expansion be the catalyst for every action that precedes that desire. Let everything I do have you in it; every seed I plant, every tree that bears fruit, every fruit that I eat and share with others. Let your love be felt in a way that I can understand it. Thank You. I love you. Amen.

-

BLESSING DECLARATION

Big G. Today I declare my blessings. I am incredibly grateful for the way in which you Grace my life and take my perceived pain away. I am alive, every day above ground is beautiful, I am grateful, for all that I am and for the ever-expanding nature of this life experience, I am safe, because I am never separate from you, I am blessed, because every experience is Divine, and I am loved, infinitely, because it is who I am, as I am of you. I am kind to myself, and as I welcome this New Year, I do it with love. I see love in everyone, everything, every experience and especially in myself. I love my sacred body, I love my skin, I love my hair, I love my face, I love my job, I love my perfect dream clients, I love to serve, I love my family, I love my friends, I love my bank account, I love adventures, I love writing, I love the sunshine, I love the beach, I love finding you in everything I do, everything I see. Because when I find you in them, I am reminded that all is well, I am on my path and my Divinity is absolute. My desires are serving because they remind me of my purpose - to expand the love that I am. As I honour myself, life honours me.

-

LOVE IS LOVE IS LOVE IS LOVE

As you allow spirit into your physical world, you will start to observe the way spirit is ever present and it's revelation is dependent on your awareness of it. I had an incredible synchronistic moment today. I was at the gym, on a machine, and next to me lay a small feather. I don't have any particular attachments to feathers, but I don't see them incredibly often, and very rarely indoors. So I noticed that it was there. And it was flying around and around, as though it were circling next to me, calling my attention. I couldn't stop looking, I was mesmerised. The angels were revealing themselves to me. They wanted me to remember that their infinite guidance, support and love was at my service. It is ALWAYS at my service, but in that moment I was receptive to the message and the reminder was ever serving. And so I decided to share that magical Divine moment with my people (on the socials), and as I pressed the share button, the music in my ears played, "we can hear the angels calling us…", as if the miracles weren't already boundless, they always confirm their presence. And because I was connected in that moment, I channeled a message from them, they said, "ask us for what you want, and so it is". We can call upon our angels whenever we desire. And although we may have specific spirit guides and protection angels, we are not limited by numbers in the spirit world, legions upon legions are always at your service. Call upon them *as though* you have an army of angels working in your corner, because you always do. You are not alone, we are eternally connected to the infinite supply of all that is.

-

Today I did a micro meditation and the most beautiful arrangement of lights and colours were revealed to me. Imagine swimming, but more so floating, in a sea of translucent pastels, with little sparkles of bright light swimming with you, and you could observe all the dimensions happening simultaneously, but not from a human perspective, instead from an energetic perspective. I could feel it all, at the same time. But it was not overwhelming, it was instead, incredibly calming. I've had similar experiences before, but it was so beautiful to feel this again. It's in these experiences that I truly remember who I am, where I'm from, and what I'm here to do. And nothing feels like too much or too heavy, because I am reminded that I am ALWAYS carried, supported, held, guided. It reminded me to zoom out, and observe from that place. Not in it, of it. Not in it, of it. Not in it, of it. But as you're of it, you're also in it. But you're more of it than you'll ever be in it. It was painless. There is only love, only harmony, only well-being. The soul is never afraid because it never forgets what it is. And in this moment I was reminded. And in this moment, so are you. All is well. You are on your path.

But after my meditation, the human part of me also acknowledges that although the spirit part of me felt an immense sense of peace, the human part of me still feels perceived pain here on earth. As humans, we empathise, we feel perceived loss and separation, we find death hard to comprehend when we are in it and having the experience exposed to us. We are often reminded of our temporary human experience. And all of that is part of our humanity. It is incredibly important. Because it is serving for our expansion. When we are reminded, we remember to love harder, to forgive quickly, as though there were nothing to forgive, we remember to live fully as often as we can. We are reminded to zoom out and see the love that exists in every person and every experience. We don't just want the spiritual experience, we chose this. We chose the human experience too. Feel the depths of it all. <3

And the prayer that followed that revelation was this;

Big G, Divine Guidance. Today I thank you. I thank you for reminding us what love is. I acknowledge that our souls feel no pain and feel no resistance to the transition between physical and spirit. That it flows so effortlessly, like a dance between two worlds, coming back into the physical for greater expansion, and then like a cosmic breath, returning to the Source once more. And today we witnessed the whole world shift off the strength of one human* - a profound expansion of love. Every temporary human experience is an extraordinary opportunity to expand. And although hearts are aching from the perceived pain of loss and separation, it's in this moment that we are reminded of our Divinity, of our Oneness, of our Universal breath. And it's with incredibly full hearts that we continue projecting that love, to those who need it, to the world, to each other. We take from one wave to give to another, and yet the ocean remains full. As I take another breath, I am reminded of what this life offers - the opportunity to expand, to experience, to create, to give… the one truth that we are - LOVE. Amen.

*Inspired by the post "The whole world just shifted off the strength of one human. Your life is an extraordinary opportunity. Never ever forget that."

-

It's our innate nature to want intimate connection with everything and everyone. We will always look for a place to feel safe within others. We are designed to see ourselves in others, because the Law of Divine Oneness, says that we are all one energy. Which means, when I search for me in you, I'm really just looking for me in me, and naturally I can

observe my own reflection, which is why so often it is easy
for us to connect with others, even complete strangers,
because we observe ourselves and make connections in our
minds that make us feel safe and recognise that reflection.

-

I've always vowed that in this book I'll be as transparent as
possible, and share things with you, that many may not
understand, but are willing to acknowledge as being a part of
my truth and my experience. And so, I share this with you
now. I have a friend who I met in Bali last year. Since our
meeting we have had a strange unexplainable connection.
She is very open as a channel and because of this she is
incredibly in tune and psychic. We learnt early on that we
had a profound energetic connection. She would often send
me messages during dream time and I would often send her
messages during dream time. At times it became
overwhelming because it was becoming more and more
frequent and it was causing tension between us in our
conscious state. So I put up an energetic wall and didn't let
her back in. When we were in close proximity (she had
visited me in Australia a few times, and stayed with me), the
connection was heightened. I recall one night, I was sleeping
on the couch, she was in my room, and at 5am I was
abruptly woken up, she was haunting me, I was scared. I

was telling her to leave me so I could sleep and she wouldn't leave me. In the morning, she says that at 5am, her and I were fighting and I wouldn't leave. This wasn't an isolated event. Another time, I received a message that she needed to take her health more seriously, so I telepathically (which is just energetically) sent her a message. She didn't send me a text message saying she received the message, which was odd because without question, every time she received an energetic message from me, she would reach out. Just by chance a few days later I was spending time with a friend who's birthday it was, and my friend called her and she was eating an apple. She didn't know that I was with the birthday girl. And I said, "did you get my message?", and she said, of course I did, I just didn't want to acknowledge it. Recently, she came to me during my dream state (please note, that we surrender during dream state and offer no resistance, so that's why our channels are so open and more receptive to this sort of connection), it was 2.22am, and I said, "what do you want? I'm tired and I need to get back to sleep and I can't while you're here". I should mention, that I often take down the "energetic wall" and let her back in because I enjoy our connection. So the wall was down at this stage. She wanted some Gee love, she needed a hug and then she left. In the morning I checked my phone and she had messaged me telling me I was in her room, but this time it was different, it wasn't just energetic, it was a full body experience. My mum had also received a missed call from her at 4am. She then mentioned that at 2.22am that's when she had decided to leave the party and go home. She often refers to me as a "wizard", because of the way her and I communicate. Why do I share all of this? Because this is possible with everyone at any time. There is no separation between you and another, in fact there is no other. The only reason her and I can send telepathic messages is because we allow it and offer no resistance. But this was our natural way of communication, before 3D conditioning placed linear time and space limitations on how we connect and communicate. When I send someone love, they instantly receive it, no time delay. The spirit part of them will receive it, and although not conscious of it, their entire energy field will have shifted. I often send strangers messages of love energetically. And I know that they are receiving the messages. It's like when you think of someone, and then suddenly they reach out. It's a vibrational frequency, moving in waves, and sending messages (transmitting information). Always flowing, always moving through each of us, because although we perceive this 3 Dimensional experience, we are in fact energetic beings. If you want to put this to the test, the best way to do it is with someone you trust and have a close connection with at first. Both intend to send each other energetic messages. And be open to removing the veil of limitations that prevent that connection. I have another friend who is also psychic (just to note; I believe we are ALL psychic, but those who identify as psychic have already removed the veil and are an open channel to the messages therefore more receptive to the messages being realised by them), and I was out the other night and wanted to send her a message and so I sent it energetically. In the morning she messaged me saying, "I feel you didn't do what we had discussed". Energetically, she had received the message, and because she trusted the intuitive message, she was able to use her conscious mind to translate the message. Start paying attention to when this is happening in your life. It will be more often than you have previously perceived.

The soul knows no bounds. I was telling a friend the other day how I everyday send a particular person love who doesn't know me, who probably never will in this time and space reality. She could not understand why I would do that. And I told her that energy knows no bounds. And the physical part of them may not hear that projection of love, but the moment I declare it, their soul feels it, their entire aura receives that love and they feel lighter. And so everyday I will continue sending them my love, because physical limitations do not account for the boundless and infinite connection of our souls - as we are but one soul.

-

LOVE IS LOVE IS LOVE IS LOVE

Love is all and all is love, and love is the highest healing frequency of all. When I "send light", this is my process. I get myself into a still place, I do a micro meditation (I can get myself to the surrendered state very quickly, because I've been doing this for so long, but be patient with yourself). I then visualise them in front of me, I see them physically (if I don't know them personally, I visualise their aura), I become them, there is a tether between their heart and mine. Then I receive light and energy from the sun, as though a powerful ray of light is beaming into my vessel and simultaneously into their vessel. I wait for as long as it takes until their entire vessel has been lit up and the energy/light is circulating around them. I know when they have received it fully because they begin to float (levitate) as though the ray of sun is drawing them up unto it. Sometimes they will do something quirky or fun which makes me laugh. I just sent light to a client's daughter, and as she floated she was dancing and it was so cute and fun! Depending on why I'm sending light, I may also use the elements. I'll hold onto a lit candle and amplify the energy as I pray over them, the flame (fire element) amplifying the energy of the light. I imagine the light start from the heart centre and filling up the entire vessel, until it pours outside of the physical (as though it were overflowing), and then I watch it shoot out like an explosion and fill their entire energy field and beyond (again, this is dependent on how much of the light they allow themselves to receive and how much overflow is available). Some people take minutes to receive the light, others take seconds. I've also had a few who don't receive it, so I have to talk to them first to soften their resistance before I can send the light. You can receive light, just by being open to letting others sending you love. I imagine myself protected by a white diamond orb, and I pray that only love can enter my field. So no one can send me bad juju. You also don't have to receive any energy from anyone else if you don't want to. To stop anyone entering your field, visualise a wall around your field, where no one can enter and declare that no one is allowed in, or even no one but those who are of love. Be mindful if you do this, because it's energy and it will be felt in the physical plane too, and it will shut people out.

-

No one rejects love. They only resist it. But they always receive it. Because it is an offering of themselves as something they can observe. You let them witness their true self. It is always received. Your love for them is their desire to be loved. It is met and received always. Even when not on the conscious level.

CHAPTER 5

WHAT GOD WANTS YOU TO REMEMBER

"In every stranger is a story the universe needed to tell." - Medusa

I love this so much. It encompasses just how grand and significant we all are. I've always said that God intends to work though you. The other day dad and I were sitting and discussing an ancient philosopher. And dad pondered how it was that this man acquired all this knowledge long before there was any technology to prove it. And my response was, "that's how God intended to work through him, that was his message to deliver". And that's how I see all people, as messengers. Now of course, not all the messages are for me personally, but collectively the messages create our web and allow for the beautiful flow of life. Even with everything happening in the world, I have observed extraordinary love and togetherness. If in doubt, just love.

Although the premise of this book is that of The Law of Attraction, many other laws exist, just like that of Gravity and Cause and Effect. Let me introduce you to the Law of Divine Oneness. The Law of Divine Oneness - everything is connected to everything else. What we think, say, do and believe will have a corresponding effect on others and the universe around us irrespective of whether the people are near or far away, beyond time and space. The way to make this easier to understand, is that we are all just extensions of each other. I am you and you are me, I am that tree and that tree is me. I am not a drop in the ocean, I am the entire ocean in a drop. So by doing good to one person means I am doing good to the entire universe. Everyone is so busy trying to change the world, start a revolution, be the catalyst for a movement, and I commend their tenacity. Really I do. But true change lies within. You only need to impact one person, to impact the entire planet. To progress forward, you only need to take one step forward. Those steps will turn into leaps, those leaps into bounds and as you gain momentum, the continuity of your progression will become exponential. You want to change the world? Smile at a stranger, help your neighbour unpack their groceries, respond to that question posted on Facebook by a friend and offer your assistance, or just love yourself. That's how you change the world, by helping one person you consequently help the entire world. You change the world by looking inwards. You change the world by being love. The more love we project the more love we receive, the more love the higher the vibration of the entire world, the ever expanding universe. It's time to remove the labels, you don't need to be this or do that. Just be. In this moment right now. Be present. My favourite quote of all time is *"je suis comme je suis"*, it means I am as I am. It's that simple. You want happiness for you? You want happiness for the world? Wipe the slate clean, remove the baggage and just bask in this moment of perfectly imperfect glory, because all is as it should be, because you are. Jason Mraz once said, "life is empty and meaningless. It's you who gives meaning to something. The world you see before you is entirely defined by your interpretation of it. Otherwise it just is." So how will you interpret your world today? How will you give meaning to that which just is? Because you are.

WHO ANSWERS YOUR PRAYERS
(Answer inspired by Abraham Hicks Talk)

Pieces of consciousness (or infinite intelligence) come through in response to the question being asked and by whom the question is asked as to their level of readiness for the answer. So the body of consciousness responding to your vibration is not always the same because each question asks for a different level of focus and thus a different level of understanding.

It is possible for us to collectively create a common consciousness (in this physical world).

Attention to something is maintenance of it. Abraham Hicks summed this up perfectly when He used the metaphor of an abandoned house. An abandoned house will deteriorate much faster than a house that's lived in, not because of any physical maintenance but because of your attention to the house.

God exists within everything. And we experience Him through our own existence. You are indeed given the gift of the Gods.

Consciousness forms matter. Consciousness creates form. Form does not create consciousness. Everything was vibration first. And everything is a vibrational interpretation.

As long as you believe in something - you create it to be as real as it can be to you. Any thought of anything that you bring into focus manifests. It first lives as vibration. And as you think, you vibrate, as you vibrate, you attract, and as you attract you receive. And there is ALWAYS more. We're all in this together - physical and non-physical. Inspired by Abraham Hicks, there is a three step process, 1. Ask, 2.

Receive (vibrationally), and 3. Allow. Allow the desire you ask for. Strong asking, and a little allowing goes a long way. Step 2 is not your work, only steps 1 and 3. And to get into a place of allowing, you must release resistance and be in alignment with your inner being. Alignment first, which leads to the intuitive action that follows. To release resistance you can start by creating good feeling thoughts, having fun, feeling joy, etc. Be satisfied with where you are and simultaneously eager for what's coming next.

Let's expand on the element of FOCUS. A soft and gentle focus will get you everything you want. That's because there's less resistance when we are gentle with our focus.

Perception altering involves the process of changing the FOCUS of your consciousness.

When you ask, you shall receive. This is law. If you embody the feeling you desire now, it's already in your possession. You decide what you want and why you want it. But not when, where, who or how. That's up to God. (And by God, I mean the part of you that offers no resistance)

And so, as this book was born, so was the idea that God is me. Let's address this now. I am not God, but God is me. God is you. God is all of us. God lives within us. We each contain the power of God. God, being the ultimate creator. *The eternal child, playing the eternal game in the eternal garden* (- Aurobindo). Most of us see separation between our human selves and God, and we assume that the only way to enter His Kingdom, is once we cease to exist in physical form and return to spirit form. But it is in this false assumption that we silence our power. Because it is not then, but now, that we have access to His Kingdom. Because He is never separate from us. He always lives within us. And our power to create as God creates, lives with us. And the pain that we often create (or more so perceive) is due to our observation of separation. Because once we realise that we are Gods reflection, we truly know, without doubt, with complete faith, that we are already saved. We are the salvation. We are the creation, the creator, the observer, the expansion, the expander, the saved and the saviour. Often this knowledge is too much to handle, because that would mean that we are completely responsible for our human experience, and it seems easier to leave it in someone else's hands. People often prefer to give their power away. But that isn't why we are here. We are here to remember that the power is ours and we can choose in every moment to use it to expand, to love, to grow, to give, to create, to experience, to live. Because it is not then, but now that we are spiritual beings having a human experience, and just as we came from God and to God we shall return, this human experience is an expression of God. And so the next time you ponder who you are, remember that you are love, and God is you.

Surrender... To truly understand the concept of surrender is difficult. Surrender itself isn't difficult (getting there is, but once you're there it isn't), but understanding what surrender is, is difficult. When you find that you are at a point of capacity; that is, you have surpassed your highest possible limit, the threshold has succumb to the pain of the experience and you couldn't possibly handle any more, many would say that this is the point in which they surrender. They get on their knees, crying to God, telling God that they are giving it all to him, begging God to intervene and help them overcome whatever resistant feeling(s) they are experiencing. But that isn't surrender. It may seem like it is, but it isn't.

This form of surrender, is asking God to intervene but still expecting a certain outcome. As in, "God please step in to help me ease the pain so that I can feel like myself again"... God I give it to you, but I still want to be healed, I still want to feel loved, I still want to feel abundant, I still want to feel whole, I still want to feel fulfilled. The concept is flawed, because it suggests that however you tried to control it, didn't work, but now you are allowing God to control it, but you are still waiting for the same outcome (i.e. a desired result).

True surrender is when you give it to God, with no expectation of the outcome. It's when I say, "God, I'm giving this to you now, if it is what I want it to be, then ok, but if it's not, if the discomfort I'm feeling right now is what I'm supposed to be feeling to evolve, to learn, then that's ok too. And although I don't want that, I will allow it, because if that's what's for me, I will allow it." Please know that I know that this is hard. I know the difficulty in truly surrendering. And that's why I also know that most people never truly surrender, because you have to walk through the fire to reach relief. And for most people, that is unbearable, they have already reached their threshold. They are already in the midst of incredible discomfort, pain, anger, frustration, and allowing more of it without resistance, isn't even something they would ever consider.

I had my moment of true surrender when I found myself bed ridden for days in agonising pain. A pain that was with me consistently for over a month (with no moment of relief). I couldn't get out of bed, I couldn't work, I couldn't work out, I just cried and cried and cried. I was at capacity. Beyond capacity. The idea of death was a better choice than that of living in that discomfort any longer. (At no point did I consider self-harm, but I asked God to take me quickly, because I didn't want to live in it any longer). I finally reached a point where I said aloud to God, "God I am giving it to you, all of it. I surrender. I surrender. But I truly surrender. If I am truly supposed to experience this, then that's ok, I don't want it, I really don't want it, I don't want to feel this, I wouldn't wish it upon anyone, I am hurting, but if I'm supposed to feel it, I will allow it. I will allow the experience because I signed up for this human condition, I signed up for this vessel, and although it doesn't feel good to me right now, if that's what it's supposed to be, then I will work through it. But if it's not what I'm supposed to experience, then inspire me to heal myself. Show me the way, show me the way, I surrender, I give it to you, I do not expect an outcome."

Leading up to this point I was doing so much controlling, I was utilising all the techniques I would recommend to everyone else to heal themselves. Meditation, visualisation, light work, healing transference, mantras, everything. Chapter One I shared my favourite healing mantra, "I am healed because I am the healer, I am healed because I am the healer", the idea that I am not God, but God is me, and if God is me, I embody all that He is, and all His power, including that of healing. But deeper than that, the idea that I am healed because there is nothing to be healed, because I'm a Divine Being, and to feel healed, I just need to remember that I am. But even with the depth of all my knowledge and my experience in spiritual teaching, nothing was working. And now I know it's because within all of those techniques, I was coming from a place of resistance to the experience and lack, the lack of health, I was expecting an outcome, expecting to be healed from pain. That means that my focus was on the pain and not on Divinity, not on health, not on God.

Once I truly surrendered, allowing myself to truly experience it, without judgment, I realised I was free from the constraints of the experience that I had placed upon myself. I woke up the next day, liberated, with health, able to function, aligned with love, free.

True surrender is giving it to God and allowing the experience to be what it is, without expectation or judgement, and without the idea that you know what is for your highest good. Because only God knows what is for our highest good, and the highest good of everyone involved. You are not your vessel, your vessel is borrowed, you honour your vessel, you love your vessel, but you are not your vessel. Your soul chose this vessel, to experience this physical condition, but it is not who you are. Who you are is spirit, is light, is love. So any human feeling and experience that doesn't feel good to you, is not in alignment with who you truly are, it is not of love, it is not of light, BUT that doesn't mean that you don't need to experience it to learn something deeper. You chose this human experience, and sometimes that comes with pain, frustration and anger, because that is part of the humanity of this journey. Sometimes you are going to feel discord, but that's what you signed up for, and that's ok. If you are supposed to experience it, then allow it. Even when you know it isn't aligned with who you truly are, even if it isn't aligned with light and love, allow the experience anyway, allow yourself to learn.

Don't mistake this for prolonged discomfort, because it isn't designed to last "forever", our forever is love. But allow it to be whatever it is in the moment.

-

We find ourselves translating "reality" as "physical". Reality is just an interpretation of vibration. All energy is real. It just so happens that certain frequencies become "physically visible" by us humans. But all energy is real. You aren't creating something that doesn't already exist. The thought alone attunes to the vibrational frequency of it. It's all real. Instead you want to come to the realisation of the frequency that you can interpret as physical form. That's all just energetic shifting. It is designed to be easy. It is the natural state of things. You don't need to discover, understand or try, you just need to allow what is.

The gut feeling is the God feeling. I get asked all the time how to know it's from God. If you feel it in your gut, it's from God. Get out of your head, spend time just allowing your intuition to guide you. It's an unexplainable feeling. There's so much sacredness in the unexplainable. The human part of us wants to put words to everything we feel. But how can words truly embody the vibration of the feeling…? How can I explain the unexplainable without morphing it's true essence…? Try less to understand, and focus more on just being what is. Joy, God, Bliss, Alignment exists for you right now. You don't need to find, try or understand. You just need to allow it.

I have been doing a lot of channeling work lately, and I can feel your call. You are asking for guidance, and as you ask, you receive. You think you aren't receiving what you have asked for, but instead you just aren't receptive to the messages. Your job is not to search for answers, but instead to tune into them. Your job is to be in alignment, have fun, feel joyous, do all the things that fill your heart up. There is nothing more you need to know. You are infinitely loved, supported and guided. The same force that you came from is the same force that guides you. You are not the created, you are of the creator. There isn't separation between you and all that is. Love is all.

I often hear people react to my messages by saying, "you keep saying the same things". Yeah I do, and that's because the truth that will set you free, and by free I mean, to remember who you already are, hasn't changed. But for you to suggest that I'm saying the same things and yet your life hasn't changed, is because the truth hasn't changed, but neither have your old belief patterns. So you are being led to where you've always been. I don't want you to be inspired. I want you to be committed. Committed to coming to the realisation of who you truly are - a DIVINE BEING, a LIGHT FILLED EMBODIMENT OF LOVE.

-

Let's talk about external validation. How are you to seek that which is outside of you, when everything is within you…? We believe that we are One with all (The Law of Divine Oneness), therefore, I am you, you are me, we are all just reflections of each other. So whatever I am observing, is just me in a different form (but really just one energy). So when I think that I am seeking validation from that person over there, I am really just seeking validation from SELF. (Mind-blowing, I know!) So you are never seeking external validation, you are just seeking validation from a part of you that you can observe, comprehend and translate, which is perceived as physically outside of you. It is literally like looking in the mirror for "approval"; but instead through people, places and experiences. But this understanding is not about the concept of external validation as much as it's about the knowing that we do not need to seek. We were born validated. Period. Your existence here in this physical plane is irrefutable proof that you are already validated, that you are already full, love, complete, whole. You are validated because you were born. You are validated because you exist. You are validated because you are of love. You are validated because you are of God. So you don't need to validate that which is already validated. Being the observers of our thoughts, we can understand that; when you seek validation from another (there are no others), you are really just seeking validation from self, and if I'm seeking validation from myself, and as an observer of my thoughts, let that remind me of my ultimate truth, and my ultimate truth is that my existence is proof that I am already validated, therefore I don't need validation, therefore I feel good, whole, complete, full, one with you, one with everyone, one with God.

PRAYER

Divine Guidance, allow me to realise the light that exists within my vessel and let me remember that I was born healed, as I came in to this world Divine and to tap into that Divinity, is merely to choose to. Allow me to see the ease in every decision. I trust my higher self to lead the way - my only job is to silence the internal chatter so that I can hear the intuitive nudges. There is nothing too big for me and everything that flows into my experience is Divinely orchestrated and simultaneously a reflection of my vibrational offering. I feel immense gratitude for your love and guidance. Thank you, I love you. And so it is. Amen.

-

There can often be disconnect between what is in your subconscious mind programmed as a belief and what your conscious mind wants to believe. We may say we want to be a certain person, or even that we are, and then we behave in a way that contradicts that conscious desire. And that's because there is discord between our subconscious belief and our conscious desire. And for most of us, we are completely unaware that this is the case. I had a conversation with a client recently who had found herself in a predicament with her partner. He was behaving in a way that didn't at all align with his (conscious) beliefs. And when she was sharing the experience with me, I shared with her this information. And it was a huge light-bulb moment for her and her partner, because now aware that the subconscious belief was *not* one that aligned with the conscious desire, he could actively work on reprogramming the subconscious mind, so that it does align with the conscious desire. Let me go a little deeper with this, so you can truly understand how it applies to our belief system and the byproduct of those beliefs; our behaviour.

So how do you know what you believe? What I mean, is how do you know what your subconscious mind holds as truth? You observe your behaviour. You can say that you believe one thing, or at least your conscious mind wants to believe that, but if your behaviour doesn't align with that belief, then your true (subconscious) belief isn't in alignment with the conscious desire. Let me give you an example. Let's say that everyday you say that money is unlimited and that you believe you live in an abundant Universe, but you simultaneously hold on tightly to money, you think things are too expensive, you worry when bills come in, you try to save money wherever you can, you always look for discounts, that behaviour suggests that your subconscious belief is that money is limited, offering a vibration of scarcity and lack. Another example is when you tell your partner that their love is enough and the only person you want to share your life with is them, on a conscious level, you believe that truth, but then you behave in a way that contradicts that conscious desire; you flirt with other people, you seek attention from others, you may even text or talk to other people, you may even cheat (emotionally or physically) (this assumes you believe in monogamy in this example). So your subconscious belief isn't in alignment with the conscious desire. And you may not even know what your subconscious belief is, but observing your behaviour allows you to observe the discord between your conscious desire and your conscious behaviour, pointing to an alternative subconscious belief. Through this self-awareness, you then have the opportunity to correct it, or more so, reprogram the subconscious mind (i.e. belief). I've provided many tools in this book on how you can reprogram your subconscious mind. But one of the most effective tools is to work with a coach, healer, energy worker, etc. Their impartiality, allows for them to observe your behaviour as someone who has no emotional attachment, and provide you with personalised tools for you to redirect and reprogram efficiently and effectively. Of course, this isn't the only way, you have everything you need to reprogram your subconscious beliefs on your own, I just know the power of utilising a coach. There's a reason that even the best athletes in the world, have coaches. Because the coach can see things that aren't in your awareness and bring them to your awareness.

-

I was recently on a phone call, someone I had just met, but what I knew of her was that she was a self-proclaimed "woo woo", just like me, and incredibly in touch with her spirituality and Divinity. Most of what she said resonated with me deeply. As I commended her on her willingness to take action on her intuitive nudges, she responded with "I don't have a choice, and besides I love not knowing". That made me reflect, I didn't respond to her, but I wrote myself a note to make sure I touched on it in this book. We are never "not knowing", as we come from the "all-knowing". Our intuitive nudges come from the higher self, the part of us that already knows. And so, to trust the intuitive nudges, is to trust the

119

part of you that already knows. Think of it like this; the physical part of you is in the valley, and in front of you, you see multiple paths, mountains, trees, large rocks, animals, the sky looking grey, and anything else that you can observe. But your higher self is on the mountain top, with a clear view of what came before you, where you are, and what is to come. And the higher self is connected to you, and is guiding you, whispering the right way to go, and when we listen, we hear the whispers, and we can trust that the higher self, knowing the path, will always guide us on the best possible path. And to listen is merely to silence our thoughts and surrender to the "gut feelings" that wash themselves upon us. But the most important element, is to then ACT on those feelings. Because the feelings alone, do not shift anything, we must use the physical body to act.

-

Akasha. Akasha is a term for a supposed all-pervading field in the ether in which a record of past events is imprinted. (Thank you Google) Now for the record, let's remove the "supposed" element of the definition, and now you know where I stand when it comes to Akasha and the Akashic Records. We ALL have access to the Akashic Records. Let's speak from a scientific perspective for a minute. Everything holds a frequency, it exists as energy, and energy cannot ever be destroyed, it can only ever be transferred and transformed. So every thought ever thought still exists as energy in the collective consciousness. And this wealthy energy field of knowledge is often referred to as Akasha. And accessing the Akashic Records is just tapping into the collective consciousness and recognising that every answer already exists, and as we are of that collective consciousness, we have access to all of it. Think any thought right now... now all of a sudden I too have access to that thought, as it's energy, and that energy is carried in the collective energy field. Some of us have an easier time accessing the Akashic Records as we are clear channels for it, and we can use the information accessed. For many, the information stored isn't necessary, because just like a photocopy, the carbon copy of what you need has already come with you. The parts of Akasha that you need have already been accessed and so you do not need to consciously access the records.

CHAPTER 6

DARKNESS IS THE RESISTANCE TO LIGHT

Contrast is not destructive - it's actually highly creative. And the constant changing form of our reality is an expression of our creation. And our perception of the contrast is what gives it meaning. But we often make it far too personal… "Why is this happening to me…?", "Why is this storm so destructive… is God punishing us…?". But our perception of "hate" (or of its likeness) is the destroyer - not the creation. The creation is a result of the perception and not the other way around.

How does the contrast serve you? It definitely serves you in some way - because you're holding onto the belief attached to it. It serves you in two ways. One; it provides some sort of satisfying feeling, even if your perception of that feeling is unpleasant. Or two, and where I'd rather you focus, it serves you because it leads to clarity of what you desire (because you're experiencing something that may feel unpleasant), and that desire leads to you asking (God) and receiving, which causes an expansion. An expansion of you and an expansion of the entire Universe. Because an expansion of you IS an expansion of the entire Universe.

And so the contrast you experience, through your own perception of an experience, leads to the expansion of the entire Universe. That alone holds immense profoundness.

Darkness does not exist on its own. It exists only through its relationship to light. Darkness is the absence of light, or better defined as the resistance to light. Much the same as pain, worry, doubt, unhappiness, resentment, or any unpleasant feeling does not exist on its own. It exists only through its relationship to well-being. An unpleasant feeling is the absence (resistance) of well-being. Well-being is always there, we are just not allowing it to flow through us. We are resisting it. Just as darkness resists the light. We too, resist our natural state of being, our innate vibrational frequency, the harmonious song of the Universe. We do this because we temporarily forget who we truly are. It happens, its in our human condition that we do this. We are surrounded by conditional thoughts. Don't be hard on yourself, it's okay. But we know better than to stay in that place of resistance for too long. We know that once we remember who we are, we remember that allowing the well-being to flow is easy. All it requires is for us to surrender. Surrender to who we really are. Surrender to the joy that this human experience brings us. We came here to smell the flowers, watch dogs play, cook, eat, go on rollercoasters, travel, explore, be. That's why we are here. We are here to forgive ourselves when we forget. We came here all-knowing, all-powerful, but if we were to never experience the human condition and the flaws attached to it, then we wouldn't have signed up, because we could be in constant harmony as spiritual beings. But instead we chose this physical experience because we wanted to rediscover our innate power. We wanted to experience the journey of becoming more of ourselves. And so it's in the darkness that we remember that there is light, we remember that the light is always there, and we are just resisting it.

MOEY

This is a story I've never told, mostly because I was afraid to tell it, but also because I couldn't put the experience into words. No words could truly express how I felt and how I was evolving. The entire experience was so much more than me - knowing that I am everything and everyone.

It was in this 10 year period that caused my most significant expansions, that clarified my desires, that brought to the surface so many harbouring truths and beliefs that I had that weren't in alignment with who I truly was.

Even writing this right now is triggering me, because I have felt immense discomfort sharing this story, but I share it now for both of us; me, to help me release, surrender and become more of who I truly am, and you, to encourage you to do the same. Know that I share this story with love and my greatest desire is that it serves you in some way.

I want to introduce you to my first year of Uni, end of exam party, stranger with familiar connections, a new friend, Moey.

I've never been able to clearly define our relationship. He's always been my best friend but also the only man I've known in my life from the age of 18 to have played such a significant role in my becoming (aside from my dad). Moey and I come from different (physical) worlds. And it was those differences that caused the most tension between us. He is a devout Muslim Australian who always puts his faith in God before everything. A quality that I admire deeply. But attached to his faith came a set of "rules" (really just conditioned beliefs) that didn't always align with my beliefs, and due to our very significant connection, caused a lot of tension between us. In hindsight I know that the tension was there to teach us more about ourselves, but lessons can only serve you if you are receptive to them. I wasn't always awake, and before I was awake, triggers would become arguments, that would become fights, that would become bad feelings, which would become my point of attraction. I was giving too much power to so much outside of me. Can you imagine what sort of a toll that had on my life; my physical body, my belief system, my emotional and mental well-being, my spiritual expression (or more so suppression). I was living by default, always reacting to my experience with negative feelings, not realising that my reactions were my creative centres for my coming experiences. Now put that on repeat...

I would often get asked about love from friends or family and it was the one topic area that I wanted to avoid completely. I wanted to put it on mute. I never had a satisfying response. The truth is that I just didn't know what to say. I knew that the fear of it stemmed from my youth - I was ALWAYS afraid to talk about boys. I was the oldest child and that often came with a weight of its own. And I fed the fear well into my adult life. Now don't get this confused with lack of love or connections, I had many, I just kept them VERY private. I'm in my late 20s and if you asked my parents if I've ever been on a date - they wouldn't be able to tell you.

Ok, so back to Moey. If I had to describe Moey to you, so that you could picture his essence, it would be simple. He is the most kind, thoughtful, caring, nurturing, funny man I know. I never asked a lot of him, but whatever I did ask was always received with open arms. And although he embodied so much love, he never used his words to express it. He was a man of action. He would do so many things that most people wouldn't. This book wouldn't be long enough for me to list all the things he did for me and my family. And yet despite our incredible connection, his pure soul and our inability to be mad at each other for too long, we still had a huge block in the way of anything more.

The chapter is still open with Moey, but it's one that I will have to let God take control of. I know what I want, I have intended and prepared for it, as for how… That's up to God. I release any resistance I have to this manifesting in a way that I feel is best, because only God knows what's for my highest good, and what's for the highest good of everyone involved.

And I know that for many of you reading, this isn't satisfying enough, but the truth is, life just is, and not everything can be more than it is. We are so programmed to give things greater meanings than are necessary. We always ponder on what something means, whether it's a sign from God, if it's telling us something deeper, and sometimes it is all of those things, and sometimes it's none of them. The truth is simple, love. That's it. See love, feel love, embody love, project love, focus upon love, become more of love, remember love. That's it.

-

So what about fear, what does fear do…? Or really any unwanted feeling…? It CLARIFIES. It serves us. Because it's in the experience of unwanted feelings that we are able to clarify what it is that is wanted. It births the desire, it allows for the expansion, that would not be possible without the resistance of well-being. So let yourself sit with the unwanted feelings because our souls yearn for the contrast so that we can fulfil our purpose to expand.

Abraham Hicks once said, "You don't need time, you need alignment", and those words couldn't sing more truth. Alignment with you brings all things and feelings wanted.

But know that we live in an all-inclusive world - focus upon anything, brings it to life, wanted or unwanted.

"I radiate health and well-being" = FOCUS is "health"
"I don't want to get sick" = FOCUS is "sickness"

Focusing on healing is a different frequency to focusing on health. Focusing on earning money is a different frequency to focusing on abundance and wealth. Focusing on attracting a lover is a different frequency to focusing on love.

That's why so many writers, teachers and guides ask you to be careful with your words, because they create the thoughts, that create the beliefs, that create the feelings, that create your entire life and experience.

-

Channeling…! How can you channel information from the infinite source (i.e. God/Universe/you know the drill)?!

You channel when you surrender, you surrender when you ask, then silence the noise that's blocking you from hearing the call. You will feel it. It's a gut instinct. For some it's through music, movies, magazines, Social Media posts, for others it's through synchronicities, number plates, street signs, symbols as you stroll through the shops, and for others it's far more direct; it can be a whisper in your ear, a sudden movement of your body, an urge to write or draw, a visit from an angel or spirit guide through your dreams, or even a visit from an angel, spirit guide or entity throughout your day or through your meditation. There is no one way to channel, it will come to each of us differently. But you know when it's from the infinite source, when the call is too loud to ignore. You cannot silence it once you have created a conducive environment for it.

For me, I ask for guidance or answers, then I focus solely on getting into alignment. Making sure I feel joy, gratitude, love, peace, happiness. Then when I'm doing things I love to do; meditation, cooking, baking, reading, at the beach, I receive streams of consciousness, phrases, paragraphs, sometimes essays filled with knowledge. My logical mind wants to believe that they come from nowhere, but I know better, I know that they come as messages from the infinite pool.

I recently channeled this message; You don't need to find light, or the path of it. Because it is who you are. So to hear the call of your soul, you need to silence the noise that blocks you from feeling it. Surrender. Light is love, and love is light. And light is God, so love is God. And God is omnipresent. So God is you. We are collectively God.

-

Channeling tools. A truth I know; God is talking to all of us at all times. The connection between you and God is absolute.

It is never silenced. But that does not mean that all of our channels are clear at all times. Some people use what I like to call "channeling tools", because it clears the channel for them. I know people that use pendulums, crystals, tarot cards, oracle cards, wands, journals, meditation, psychedelic drugs, spirit guides, angels, ancestors, mediums, psychics, and a whole host of others, as conduits for the Divine messages. That doesn't mean that they can't receive the messages without those tools, because they can, but they feel clearer when they use the tools. And that's ok. So for some, simply asking and then receiving isn't something that is programmed as a belief within them, but asking, using a tool for guidance, taking intuitive action and then receiving, feels better to them. For me, I talk to God directly. When I have something to say, I go straight to Big G. But even if I were to "talk" to my spirit guides or even cast with a crystal in my hand, God is all, therefore I am still talking to God directly. So if you feel better using the tools, use them. The request/message isn't watered down, because you are always talking to God and God is always talking to you.

-

Resistance comes with you wherever you go. It doesn't disappear just because you change your environment. Yes, some environments are more conducive to aligned experiences, but alignment exists everywhere, it exists everywhere, because it resides within you, it's born from within, and it's suppressed from within. And leaving one place because it causes resistance, hoping to find peace in another will not bring you peace. It may for a little while, but eventually the resistance you suppressed, the resistance you didn't want to work through, will creep up on you again. As Dr Joe Dispenza says, you can't change matter with matter. As soon as you look within and work on what resists alignment, then you will transmute that vibrational offering to every room you walk into, to all the environments you reside in. You bring the light with you. I'm aware that everyone has their own energy field, but no one else's field can effect you, unless you willingly allow it. Make your energy field so strong, so filled with love, so filled with light, that when you walk into a room, everyone else's frequency changes.

-

REVELATION

God Consciousness lives within each of us, Gaia is no exception, transmuting that frequency. The only difference is that nature doesn't resist it. It flows as it is. That's why utilising nature in your spiritual practice allows you to harness the ultimate physical form of God Consciousness.

That's why we see the power in water blessings, nature circles, forest immersions, and healings using plants.

PRAYER

Divine Guidance, everything I do leads to clarity, everything I say leads to alignment, everything I feel leads to a higher vibrational offering, and I know that all of that is because you work through me. My Divinity is certain, and the only thing I need to do in the present moment is feel the magnitude of gratitude for that which I am, for that which you are. And I am receiving all the time, just like the rivers are ever-flowing, so are the energetic currents that are flowing to me, through me, for me, from me. There is one truth - and that truth is the part of me that I now intentionally allow in. Thank you. I love you. Amen.

-

Knowing the spiritual premise of everything, and acknowledging the Divinity of everything, every person, place, experience, does not discount the trauma, injustices, imbalance and pain that is felt all over the world. We can't use our spirituality to discount someone else's perceived pain, because their perceived pain, whatever it is, is there's to feel, and it feels very real to them, therefore making it valid. It's easy for me to say that the soul of the child that doesn't have food to eat today chose this physical experience to learn love and transcend, but that is Spiritual Bypassing. I take away my own responsibility. Although I am not personally responsible for anyone else, I can use my blessings to serve others, to love others, to honour others. This includes bringing awareness to the injustices that exist in the world, this includes sharing my own wealth, this includes dedicating my time to uplifting humanity so that we can all use the knowledge of spiritual enlightenment to better ourselves and our personal realities. This is acknowledging the perceived pain of the physical experience while simultaneously being aware of the Divinity of everything. I am vegan, not because I don't think that even the souls of animals chose their experience, because I do believe that, it is ALL Divine, but I am vegan because to honour what I am, which is love, is to express love to all things. I cannot eat an animal and simultaneously believe that that is an act of love. It's not the truth for me. I refuse to use spiritual bypassing to validate my immoral behaviour towards animals. Now, as I write these words, know that this is the internal process I went through to feel good about my PERSONAL beliefs. What is truth for you is valid. One of my highest virtues is to honour freewill. What feels good to you is ok. I am just sharing an example of how many often use spiritual bypassing to discount the pain of others. We should not argue the validity of pain, but rather acknowledge that it feels real to someone or something, and that realness means that it deserves to be talked about, to be shared, to be acknowledged. And no pain is greater than another. It's all subjective. And all valid. The shadows bring awareness to the desire for light.

-

Unconscious Creation vs Conscious Creation
We are always creating, expanding, becoming more of ourselves. This will always happen, it's the design. But often we unconsciously create. We don't intend, we just have experiences we don't enjoy, which reveals discord, which plants a seed of desire (of what we would rather experience) and then, depending on the vibration we are offering, we attract a new moment of physical manifestation (i.e. realisation of what is). For many, when we experience something we don't enjoy, our focus remains on the

experience we don't enjoy, for example, "I wish I wasn't stuck in traffic". My attention, focus and *intention* is on being stuck in traffic. That is my vibrational frequency. I am still creating, I'm just unconsciously creating more of what I don't desire to experience. Instead, once we experience something we don't enjoy, revealing the discord, then planting the seed of desire of what we would rather experience, we can then shift our focus, attention and *intention* to the desired outcome, offering a vibration that is different from the initial revealed discord. This is conscious creating. I experience what I don't want, revealing what I do want, and then matching the frequency of what I do want, so to consciously create. And by creation, I am referring to expansion. Because the thought alone offers a frequency, so we aren't necessarily creating more of what isn't, but rather expanding what already is, often in different forms.

-

So during a meditation recently, God revealed the concept of Energy Transference. I always knew of energy being transferred from one thing to another (that's the design), but this was a new perspective on a personal experience that I will share with you now. I am extremely sensitive to food. My body will tell me almost instantly if something sits well or it doesn't. White refined sugar almost always effects me. I swell and get an extremely sore belly. And I have always just believed that it was because sugar is heavily toxic. Until this revelation. As I was channeling, a message came through. My Human Design profile is a Reflector. If you know nothing about Human Design (this book will not cover Human Design), all you need to know is that it's extremely rare to be a Reflector and you're basically a sponge for energy. I take on energy everywhere. So I work hard to protect my energy field, but it's not always easy or possible. And what came through during my meditation was the energy transference that comes from food. The more processed the food, the more hands that have touched it. And as I eat, I take it all on. So imagine that a chemist, responsible for creating the preservative, goes to work frustrated with something that happened at home and as she's working on a chemical her energy is projected into that. Then the farmer is worried about the drought as he's packing the bananas. And then the worker at the cacao farm feels overworked and undervalued, again projecting that energy into the cacao beans. And so on and so on and so on. Then all of that energy is transferred and respectively stored in the food we consume. Packaged and processed food is heavy. Not just because of the toxins but also because of the toxic energy that isn't yours to carry. You literally are what you eat. I'm not saying to stop eating processed food, but I am saying to be mindful of what goes into your body. Because energy transfers, and when I take in so much toxic energy, I then store that energy, and either project it or feel it deeply. For me, I feel so much heaviness when I eat processed food, as though I'm carrying extra physical weight, and it is painful. I have had so many tests in my lifetime, thinking that it was a physiological problem, to no avail. Because all along it was about energy. But now that it has been brought to my conscious awareness, I can be more mindful with the choices I make about what goes into my body everyday. And I can also consciously bless and bestow love and light to everything I eat, amplifying the positive energy that resides within it. This same principle applies to people you surround yourself with, lovers you let into your energy field, books you read, content you consume, etc. But why food is such a significant one, is because we all eat everyday, and just one meal can be touched by thousands of hands. And that can be heavy.

-

The earthly, 3 Dimensional experience doesn't offer us pain, it's the thoughts attached to the interpretation and perception of the experience that creates the perceived pain. So the conflicts we experience are always internal and personal. And that's also why it is never anyone else's responsibility to change the way we feel, because feelings come from us, so it is only us who have the power to change a feeling within us. Every experience is neutral, it is not negative or positive, it is our own thoughts attached to the experience that sway it to one end of the spectrum. Instinctively any experience that evokes a sense of joy is considered a positive experience, and any experience that evokes sadness, worry, fear (or feelings alike) is considered a negative experience. Those instinctual connections will remain even after reprogramming of our subconscious minds, but what can shift are the feelings evoked from every experience. If I were to come from a place of gratitude during every experience, gratitude being a higher vibrational frequency, then my instinctual feelings will always have me perceive my experiences as positive. And no emotions should be feared or categorised as negative. Uncomfortable feelings reveal the discord, which is serving. We are eternal spiritual beings having a temporary earthly experience, the absolute truth that comes with us during every experience is always accessible. We don't need to search for the truth, the truth is already revealed, as it came here with us, we just have to come to the realisation of it.

CHAPTER 7

DIVINITY

REFLECTION

Every single day when I receive signs from God (synchronicities, my totem, my desires, messages through movies and songs, etc.), I hold up my index finger and middle finger side by side (like a closed peace sign because some believe that our fingers should be connected to represent togetherness and not separated). And I say out loud, "Thanks Big G". Each time acknowledging that God has my back and wherever I am and whatever I'm doing, God is there with me. However random it may seem, God is already there waiting for me. Don't ever doubt that God is with you. Because He is. Always. And if you have a question, just ask, and He will answer it. Always. You are loved. You are supported. You are infinite.

DIVINITY

"You decide the meanings of things and how they shape and affect you." -Amy Fiedler

I often work with people who ask me, "so this happened, what does that mean?!" And the answer is, what does it mean to YOU? How does it make you feel? What does it make you want to do? It's all relative. I choose how things impact my life and what meaning I will draw from them. There are no good or bad events in my life, there's just a series of events that I get to choose how I feel about them.

When you imagine - can you imagine ANYTHING? Like a mirror, where the reflection is instantaneous, so too is our lives, reflected from the vibration we emit. We are the reflection looking unto itself.

Ascension is not linear; you do not rise. Ascension is spherical; you expand. That is our purpose here; creative expansion.

Just as time is not linear. We perceive time as past, present, future. But just as you can think of your memories, and re-experience the feelings of those moments through the current focus and embodiment of that memory, so too can you think of your future self through your visualisations and experience and embody the feelings that you feel in those moments. You experience both the past and the future now. Time is not linear. Time is receptive to our focus. It's our focus on a moment that gives it life.

ABRAHAM HICKS INSPIRED

"Isn't it enough that you have the energy that creates worlds flowing through your fingertips."

We all have Divine paths, but we also have free will. And our free will will determine what is Divine for us. We will always do what we need to do on this physical plane, you can never get it wrong. But the physical experience will be determined by our choices, our leaps, our beliefs, our feelings, our expression. Your life will always look how you want it to look. However, this "want"/desire may come from a subconscious place, so you may not be intentional with your desire. The perception of your life will always align with your subconscious beliefs. And ultimately so will your choices. You can be intentional about your life experience, you can reprogram your subconscious beliefs so that they align with the life you desire. You can literally become your Divine Self in this physical world, by aligning yourself with beliefs that feel good, that feel like well-being, like ease, like flow. This won't necessarily come easily, you will have to work at it, you will have to experience the ebb and the flow. You have to be willing to surrender to your higher self and shed your old beliefs; the beliefs that have been conditioned upon you from this world and from the worlds before you. There will be times that you make natural progress towards your higher self, and then there will be times that you will be resisting the change. Honour it. Both are necessary. Because when we resist, we grow, we grow by being conscious of the feelings we don't want, instantaneously determining what we do want, creating a desire, causing ourselves and the entire Universe to expand. There is nothing more required of you then to just be. Your Divinity doesn't need to be earned, it needs to be realised. To come from the Divine suggests that the Divine isn't separate from us, it will always live within us. And we have access to that infinite Divine power, whenever we choose to call upon it. But we must first realise that its there. Imagine a wizard who lived his whole life not knowing he has magical powers. That's so many of us. Wizards, without realisation of our infinite power.

I want to add a deeper understanding of free will at this stage. We all have free will, but sometimes that free will has been exercised in past lives. Just as some of our free will, in this current life experience, will see the effects in future lifetimes. We need to remember the holistic perspective, it isn't just here and now, although it is always here and now, there were here and nows in past lives that planted seeds that have us eating fruit we didn't know we planted. This is how you find the balance between "Destiny" and "Conscious Creation". We have soul contracts that came from free will exercised in other lifetimes and as spirit, and we simultaneously have the free will to expand the way we desire to expand, to learn the lessons in creative and fun ways, and to even deny the lessons (but if we do this, they will come back again until we learn them - our soul wanted to transcend the lessons). But how you expand is up to you. You don't have to be anything specific, you don't have a career path assigned to you, you have the free will to decide how the messages move through you. Your purpose is to expand. That is absolute.

DANAYRA

Where can I even start. I met Danayra online many years ago. She was a Beta Tester for my first ever online course (from my previous business), and as soon as we met, we clicked. It wasn't until I released an online article that got published to the Huffington Post that we really started to connect. (She's originally from the Bronx, and my article was about rap music, and she vibed with it).

Danayra and I had a coaching session together, chatted as friends together, for many years we would speak weekly. We built our businesses together, we shared our struggles, our resistance, our setbacks, and we worked through them together.

She believed in me even before I believed in myself. She honoured my work, she saw my value, she showed me so much love and support and it honestly fuelled me to be better. To grow into myself and my potential.

I will never forget the day that she asked me to coach her, "officially" and she wanted to pay my $5000 fee. I offered her a discount (she was my dear friend, honestly I would have done it for free), but she insisted that she pay the full amount. My gratitude could never be truly explained. Because in that moment not only did she honour me and my work, but she honoured herself, she wanted to invest in herself, and that inspired me so much. During the 3-month package (I extended our time together), she accomplished more than we had intended for the last 4 years. As for me, her willingness to work as hard as she was and to take my direction, inspired me to take so much action, that I saw my business grow more in that 3-month period than it had in the previous 2 years.

There are people that you will meet in your life that are part of you. We are all connected, that I know, but there will be a few people that your soul just remembers. Danayra is my soul sister. I treat her like I do my sister. I am so grateful to have her in my life and to share with her things that I have never shared with anyone.

She has offered to have me live with her, to support my growth, to collaborate with her. Without her, this book would have never come to be. Danayra knew me when we both just had ideas in our mind that we wanted to birth and bring to life. We didn't have an audience or content, or a platform. She was with me through the entire journey, and she treated me like I was already everything I wished to be. She saw that in me, and I will forever be grateful for that.

Humans that are just pure light beams who embody love in every moment, even when those moments are not in alignment, even when they doubt their own innate power, their own Divinity; they teach you. They teach you how to be more of yourself. Danayra has taught me how to embody my Divine Oneness with God. Even when she was in the depths of her own darkness, she never questioned her Oneness with God. Even moments when she questioned herself, she never questioned her Oneness with God. That sort of faith moves you. Even when she couldn't move forward with her own spiritual practice, she never questioned her Oneness with God. And if in her moment of darkness she was able to embody her Oneness with God, then who was I, a child of God, ever to question my own Oneness with God. If my sister is one with God, so am I, so are you. And the only time we experience the disconnect is when we let our ego speak in place of our spirit. But the connection can never be broken, just as a wave could never be broken from the ocean.

D, I love you, I see you, I am you. Thank you, from my whole heart.

-

Let's talk about Conviction. Often we ask as though we don't believe God will follow through. We live in a desire state. We believe it's possible for some, that's why we ask, but that it's likely not to happen for us. This vibrational offering will never bring you your desired reality. Your thought plan precedes its material realisation. The perfect analogy for this is; imagine you are at the grocery store, and you put into your basket everything you wish to purchase. You fill up your basket, excited about going home to experience all the things, imagining what you will cook, what you will taste, what's coming. And when you're ready, you go to the counter and you leave everything at the check out and walk out because you don't believe you have the currency to pay for everything in your basket. And then you feel resentment when you go home and don't have all the things that you invested time into putting into your basket, and you blame the grocery store for not following through, when in fact, it was that you hadn't realised the currency living in your pocket. God is the grocery store, and your faith/thought/beliefs are the currency. If I have $100 in my pocket, I shop as though I do. If I have $0 in my pocket, I act as though I do. Ask God, He supplies, but then you have to pay through your belief (i.e. your vibrational offering) and your embodiment of that which you ask for. So if you ask for abundance, you have to act like you have the currency for it in your pocket already. You need to walk, talk, act, follow through, as though it's already your present state of being. If you walk, talk and act like you maybe have the currency for it, then that doubt, that resistance, will bring forth a reality that is without conviction. Conviction, knowing, is the ultimate expression of undeniable faith that God will do His part to bring forth your desires. Wanting is believing "I do not yet have", and that comes from a place of lack, from a disconnect with God. It's not of Oneness. Oneness is knowing that you are ALWAYS connected to the Divine and infinite supply of God. You are of God. That supply is unlimited. You don't need to want what you already have. Just alter your vibrational offering, alter your frequency to match what you desire. If you want abundance, pay through the currency of abundance (i.e.

embodiment of abundance), if you want health, pay through the currency of health, if you want love, pay through the currency of love. You need to identify with the consciousness of your oneness with the infinite supply. Conviction is the absence of resistance. Conviction is not forceful (because forceful action is resistant action, it's moving forward with the belief that it's not yet so), conviction is a magnet - drawing unto itself whatever currents live within it.

The truth is, within this book I've outlined many different explanations of the same idea. That you hold an energetic current; it lives within you, it surrounds you, and it flows from you, and everything that matches that current is drawn unto it, and that becomes your reality. Your current (i.e. frequency) is determined by your dominant thoughts, beliefs and feelings; these are programmed in your subconscious mind, and your conscious mind behaves according to those beliefs. If you desire to change your physical reality, you must first alter your energy (thoughts/feelings/beliefs, which will precede your actions and behaviour). The simplest way to reach your desired state is through alignment; that is, connecting to the place within you that is pure love and well-being. To simplify; be happy and filled with joy as often as you can. Have fun, be a kid, don't attach to conditions, expectations and identities. Remember that you are pure light, that you are of God, that your connection to the infinite supply of God is ALWAYS turned on. Know that there are many tools that you can use to help you on this journey, to guide you, but the only one you ever truly need lives within you, and that is, your own Divinity.

-

I don't just believe in the Divinity of myself. I also believe in the Divinity of things, people and experiences.

God is not the creator. He is the source of creation.

His omnipresence is absolute.
If you believe that you are divinely connected to that source, then you simultaneously believe that we all are. You believe in the Divinity of all people, places, experiences and energy.

That means that if you hurt another you are directly hurting yourself. Not indirectly. Directly. Because there is no separation.

Everything is of source. Everything. Every planet, every alien, every dimension, every universe, everything. Therefore it is all Divine.

And every limit, condition and false belief you have is an illusion. It is never made real because only truth can be real. But the illusion feels real because you choose to live as though it were.

There is one absolute truth. And no one knows this absolute truth, or maybe one person does, but that doesn't matter here. Each of us are just trying to interpret that absolute truth in the best way we can. No one person is supposed to know it all, it isn't how we are designed. You do not need to know how the plants grow, how the planets move, how the organs function, how light travels. You just need to discover your own resonance with the truth, and let it become your truth. Because your truth creates your reality. Your interpretation of the ultimate truth becomes your version of this physical plane, and your truth does not need to resonate or mirror anyone else's truth, it just needs to feel good to you. We live in a 3 Dimensional world where many truths exist; different religions, different belief systems, different morals, different ideas, different cultures. And that's because there are billions and billions of versions of the ultimate truth, some overlapping, and some not. Each truth adds to the collective truth, and the collective truth isn't the ultimate truth, it's just another interpretation of it, but it is how we perceive this world.

I was once told by my dear friend Danayra, during a reading, that I know the unknown. And if I had to describe what I know in any which way, it would be that way. I just understand it, I can't explain why, nor do I need to know why, I just know. And that is enough. I also know that what I know is my interpretation of the absolute truth and there will always be parts of the absolute truth that I'll never be able to interpret. Let's use my favourite style of teaching here; a metaphor. Say you're watching a French film. And throughout your life, through your experiences, your level of understanding, along with what you've learnt, you are able to understand a few short French phrases. You are watching the movie, and suddenly you hear a phrase that you can translate and understand. Our relationship with the Universe works in much the same way. The Universe is the French film in this scenario. All the messages are there, everything that there is to ever know is being sent to us, constantly. But we are only receptive to the parts of the messages that we can recognise and translate. So we can't assume that the three lines that we have been able to translate make-up the ultimate truth, sure it is a part of the truth. But it's only the part we were able to translate. The translation may also be reliant on context. Also like language translation, when we translate from French to English, we may misinterpret some of the words and meanings and relay the translation incorrectly, this can also happen when we translate messages from the Universe. This is also because we are trying to translate the untranslatable; we are using words to describe energy, that can't truly be understood by words. Because words are limited. There is no one person that knows the absolute truth, but each of us are trying to interpret the absolute truth, and there may be overlaps, and there may be misinterpretations, but what's certain is that each of us receive exactly what we need to, when we need to. You never have to worry if the answers will come, because they already have. You will just be receptive to them when you're ready in this time and space.

-

What it feels like to be triggered and how to work through it…

So this week I've had a hell of a week. And for the record, my reference to "hell" is merely my own construct of it, it's less of a place and more of a prolonged feeling (or a collection of feelings) of overwhelm, sadness, depletion and disconnect. It has resulted in a massive introspection, which caused me to completely retreat for a few days. As in, I did not want to talk to humans. It was between God and I, and I just couldn't bare the thought of sharing the experience with another human being. One of my beliefs (although limiting, and aware of that limit, still binding in my subconscious programming), is that if I'm not in alignment, then I don't want to be around others, because I know that that often creates a bench mark for how the room will feel. So I make it my mission to find whatever has me resisting my own alignment and move past it, and if that isn't possible, I instead try to reconnect with the part of me that is already in alignment (I do this by doing high vibrational activities - things that bring me joy). So I wasn't prepared to share my darkness with anyone else, and not because I had attached shame to my experience, quite the opposite, because being aware of my darkness and acknowledging that it wanted the stage for a moment, I wanted to give it the space to have the stage and teach me.

So what happened?
I was on a Candida Cleanse Protocol, the details of the cleanse are less important for this story, but basically I was putting my body through an intense change and as everything (in my body) tries to cope with these intense changes, you can imagine that my hormones, my emotions and my physical body were taking a beating. And so it was, that I was feeling as though I was being thrown from one end of the sea to the other end. Tired, depleted, in pain* (physically)*(*pain is me resisting my own well-being, but that is always true upon retrospection, and when you're in it, that*

pain, although an illusion, feels very very real.), emotionally unstable and irritable. All of that being so, I knew I could get through it, but the triggering occurred from my relationship with my body. I come from a history of eating disorders. Specifically body dysmorphia and binge eating disorder, and I worked really hard to reconnect my mind and body, and it worked. But sometimes, when I'm not at my A-Game and I'm feeling vulnerable, I can have moments where I forget my own Divinity. This was one of those moments. I forgot how perfect I was (am). I saw someone in the mirror that wasn't me, I felt a huge disconnect and I was triggered because I thought I should look different. None of that is true, and certainly not my truth, but we are experiencing the human condition, and for me to say that any one of us is exempt from triggering thoughts, would be a lie. And I am no exception.

And so I did what I know to do. I spoke with God. I meditated. Not guided. I just put on a soundtrack of the ocean (a place that gets me into alignment real quick), and I laid there until my mind was silent. This happens really quickly for me... usually. But it took a hot minute, and by hot minute, I'd say roughly 10 minutes to silence my thoughts. But once I was there, the "God Switch" (I have talked about this elsewhere in this book) was ON! I spoke of my feelings, as though God didn't already know, but God is me, what I feel, He feels. And I asked specific questions to help me move through my perceived pain. I asked what I should do to reconnect with my body. I asked about the cleanse. I asked about business. I asked about whatever came through. No more, no less. And all the answers were revealed. And I took them all on board. I came back to my conscious state knowing that I had received and translated everything that I needed to serve me. And I took action straight away. I changed what I needed to change. I applied what I needed to apply. I removed what I needed to remove. I looked at my perceived pain and I sent it love. This action, although intuitive action, is better described in this situation as acting out of faith. I fully and completely trusted the Divine revelations and guidance provided to me. I didn't question its validity, I just knew that it was of God. It was of the all-knowing. And I didn't let my ego take the wheel after the revelations. That doesn't mean I wasn't still very willing to play with my demons. I always am. In fact I encourage that. But play as I may, I will not ever let my demons come before my truth, that God is me, I am of God and therefore Divinity is my birthright, and that knowing will always lead me to where I need to go.

I was also called to do a "spell", and I don't mean a cauldron kind of spell (although I'm not at all opposed to that kind of magic), but one that required a bottle of water, some mantras and clear intention. And after that spell, I felt something energetically completely shift for me. (Please note that my kind of magic has to always align with my two non-negotiables; it has to be of love and it cannot take away someones free will)

And with that I moved through my triggering experience and fell back into my natural state of being - alignment. It took three days. It took as long as it needed to take.

-

Faith or fear. You can't feel both simultaneously, you must choose. Fear is always perceived fear. It is only made to feel real because we focus upon it. And that focus gives it life. However, when we fear, we are in that moment, resisting our faith. Because you can't feel both faith and fear simultaneously. Faith is to know that there is nothing to fear, because we are Divinely supported and held. And that there is one truth - our absolute Divinity. And that nothing is out of reach. To have faith is to not let our internal world be effected by our external world, and instead have our internal world change our perception of the external world. When I come from a place of faith, I make decisions based on that faith, on knowing that I can never get it wrong, that nothing is too grand, that nothing cannot be realised. My Divine path is certain. But that doesn't mean that we won't experience fear, we are human, and this human experience includes that of contrast. We resist what we are so that we can be reminded of what we are, and step into that expansively. So when we experience fear, we have the opportunity to be reminded of our faith, of our innate Divinity.

DIVINITY

PRAYER

Divine Guidance, I call upon you to command the release of any resistance I may be holding on to, allow me to shift more closer to my truest self, to release any attachment to lack or poverty and realise my innate abundance and prosperity. I welcome my every-flowing creative expression and the stream that follows that expression. I ask that you ease any resistance that exists within my vessel and give me the strength I need to move through it. I shower my body with love - and may you amplify that love to Godly proportions. I call upon you to shift my awareness from fear to faith - knowing that I am Divinely Guided and eternally led to the light. May all my intentions be of love and grow from love, to love, for love, through love. And may I always find my way back home to you. I love you. And so it is. Amen.

-

So let's assume that the knowing is absolute. Let's assume that you are certain that you are of God, and that God is you. You may have this absolute knowing, and still be denying God. You can know, with certainty, who you are, and simultaneously deny that part of you, and not live up to that knowing. For example, you can know that you are really great at your job as a teacher and yet not show up as a great teacher everyday. We have to consciously live up to the knowing and belief that is within us. The actions need to support the belief. Often those actions are habitual and do live up to the belief, but when it comes to action that is not habitual, this can be a little more difficult. I can know that I am of the infinite supply and that the Universe is abundant, and when it comes to my habitual behaviours, align with that truth, but when it comes to new action, I can still find myself falling into action that is not aligned with that truth. For example, I can spend abundantly on groceries every week, and yet when I find myself needing to repair my fridge, fall into a lack mentality. We use self-awareness to observe the thoughts, feelings, beliefs and actions. Then we use our focus to create new thoughts, feelings and beliefs, mostly through repetitive exposure (so to create alignment with the Universe). Then once we have programmed our subconscious mind, we continue using self-awareness to observe whether our new actions are aligning with our belief system. But here's the kicker; we need to make sure that our willingness to be, matches our desire to be. I've said this before. You have to be willing to live up to the you that you know you are, and not just desire to be the you that you know you are. You know you are of the Divine, therefore Divine, so are you willing to show up as a Divine Being everyday? Or will you deny that part of yourself, and then feel discord because your spirit knows its Divinity, and even the conscious physical part of you knows its Divinity, and yet your conscious physical self is not showing up as that Divine being by denying their own Divinity (and hence, not taking action on that Divinity). This is important to showcase, because belief doesn't just manifest into physical. The Universe speaks vibration. I need to believe AND then become. You become before you realise (i.e. come to the realisation of all that is - your desires). So; step one, believe, step two, become (show up and live up to the truth that you know with certainty), then, step three, realise, all that is (anything you desire), as physical manifestations.

-

Recently the world has witnessed a series of natural disasters (I won't be specific here as I don't want a linear timeline to cast a bearing on the way you receive this book). But beneath the shadows of the contrast the world is experiencing, many opinions have risen to the surface, each wanting a moment on the stage. I have witnessed miracles, pain, fear, philanthropy, love, and a whole spectrum of other grand gestures. Some are referring to this as a spiritual destruction to force us to rebuild from a place of light, others are showcasing proof of doomsday, others are blaming because projecting their fear is all that makes them feel safe right now, and others are hitting social media and the streets to protest and fight for climate change, political change and agriculture change to bring awareness, to raise money and to actively participate in the unfolding of a new world. And all of these things are to be commended. I have even witnessed an incredible amount of spiritual bypassing within the spiritual community, again because bringing awareness to the physical reality of the crisis, triggers fear, and many don't know how to handle fear, and instead find comfort in light, love and optimism. But there has been a common theme that I have witnessed, and that is many are still coming from a very 3 Dimensional place when they address the possible solutions for this world crisis. How can we be proactive, how can we prevent this, how can we fix this, where should we spend our money…? Again, all very great questions to ask. But the solution has already been provided, and all those who channel regularly, already know. This is an energetic problem. We are disconnected to our Mother (the earth). We are out of alignment. We are so deep in the matrix and the 3 Dimensional programming, that we have forgotten that we are spiritual beings. Bringing awareness to the crisis is important, because it evokes feelings. I don't want to see people, animals and the earth dying, but by witnessing it, I feel called to take ACTION, to make a difference. And then I do that in two ways; one, I take immediate physical action, I donate my money, I donate resources, I spread awareness, I think of ways I can personally get involved, I completely eliminate the use of animal products (I am already vegan, but I am speaking from a general perspective here), I reduce my use of single-use plastics, I travel less, I use my car less, I do what I can to reduce my carbon footprint, and then there's the second thing I do; I reconnect spiritually, I see this as a 4th and 5th Dimensional disconnection. I pray, I send light, I project love, I give reverence to the Mother, I honour the Mother, I ask her for co-existence, I use my knowledge of energy and vibration to offer a frequency that is aligned with harmony, I spend time with the Mother, I see and feel no separation between me and ANYTHING (not just another, but anything), I come together with my brothers and sisters and hold prayer circles, I make offerings to the Mother, I cradle Her as she has always cradled me, reminding myself that She doesn't need me to thrive, but I need Her to survive. And I do all of this knowing that the Divinity is absolute, there have been no mistakes, all is as it should be, and the unravelling is teaching me, teaching you, teaching all of us. The earth is responding to the collective energy offering. We are disconnected, but we are now aware of this disconnection and have the opportunity to reconnect. There is no one to blame, no need to project our perceived pain and fear and no need to fight each other on who is more right than the other. But we have a responsibility. We have a responsibility to collectively shift our energy offering to one that aligns with love and harmony. It isn't just what I do as one, it's what we do together. But as I shift, we all shift. And so I ask you to look deep within yourself and find the place where you are disconnected, and once aware, take action to reconnect.

So wherever you are in the world, and whenever you read this, let's make an intention of light together. Let's take a moment to close our eyes and visualise white light surrounding the planet, and with me declare; *"Divine Guidance, I call upon you to shower your sacred love and light upon us. May we feel ever connected to each other and to the Mother that feeds us, protects us and lets us breathe through Her. Let us remember that we are not separate from Her, and that as she thrives, we survive. May the love that we are, and the love that exists within us be enough to heal all wounds, and not the wounds of the Mother, because we acknowledge that the Mother is not broken, but instead the perceived wounds that we observe. May love dissipate all perceived pain. We are grateful. And so it is. Amen."*

-

Manifestation versus intuition. A question that comes up often is how to determine when your intuition is guiding you versus when you are focused upon something and then unconsciously applying the Law of Attraction and manifesting that outcome through your vibrational offering. And here is my take on this: it may seem complex, but let's start here, you are of God, and one Source, and so everything that resides within that Oneness is of the Divine. There is one collective consciousness, and even in your physical form, you are still more spirit than you are physical.

Ramona Maharishi says, "In truth, you are Spirit. The body has been projected by the mind, which itself originates from Spirit. The Self is the one Reality that always exists, and it is by the light of the Self that all other things are seen."

Manifestation comes from where you focus your attention, the thought, which leads to the feeling, which leads to the vibration, which becomes your point of attraction. The thought which leads to manifestation is of the conscious (active mind). The beliefs which lead to the thoughts come from the subconscious mind, and the conditioned programming that has come from your life experience in the physical. We can consciously reprogram the subconscious mind, planting new thought seeds and creating new neural pathways which lead to new active habitual thoughts (which then impact our conscious thoughts). Then there is your all-knowing higher self, the unconscious (I know I have referred to this as your subconscious in this book, but consider this a more "scientific" perspective), the self that offers no resistance to all that is. This is where an intuitive nudge comes from. When we surrender and silence our conscious thoughts and conditioned programming, we hear the revelations that come from our intuition. You know that I believe in the Divinity of everything, everyone and every experience, and thus I simultaneously believe, that whether I believe it is a manifestation, or whether I believe it has come from an intuitive place, it is still as it should be, and holds the Divinity that I am. But how it transpires is up to you. The lessons (that lead to expansion), that our souls signed up for, will present themselves regardless of the experience. They come in many forms. We get to choose whether they come from the path of least resistance (Abraham reference), or whether we take a more imposing path. Let's say there's a mountain to climb in front of us. The mountain is the lesson, and our soul desires to get to the other side, in fact, it is what we signed up for in this lifetime. I can observe the mountain, and use my conscious mind to see it as a difficult path, and therefore my point of attraction is that the path is difficult, and through manifestation, so it is. Or, I can observe the mountain I must climb, to learn the lesson, that will appear regardless of my life path, and surrender to it, and allow it into my experience, and ask for guidance when my mind is still, and my intuition will guide me to the easiest path over or through the mountain. The lesson will remain, but how you experience it, is up to you.

A great example is this; I went to high school with a girl who was born on the same day as me, same hospital, 30 minutes apart. We lived no more than 500 metres from each other, both raised in a Greek family. According to our birth charts, our life would look the same on paper. When you look at our life experience (in this lifetime), it would also look very similar, we went to the same school, had the same friends, lived in the same neighbourhood and were raised in a similar family dynamic (both European parents, still married, one younger sibling), and yet, we couldn't have been more different. Growing up, before I immersed myself in spirituality, it made me discount astrology, because her and I were proof that the stars and planets didn't equate to the same life. But now I realise, that my soul signed up for different lessons than hers did in this lifetime. She was also not into spirituality at all. Her soul wasn't ready for these revelations in this lifetime. And that's ok. But my point is that, your unconscious (also referred to as superconscious) higher self, knows what it is here to do, and your intuitive guidance will come when you silence your conscious mind. But whether you tap into your intuition or you don't, the lessons will present themselves anyway. So you don't need to understand any of this, but if you do understand it, you can navigate your way through this life experience in a much more intentional way.

Here's another interpretation:

When I first started this journey, however you choose to define it. I came to a cross roads. I had the understanding that I created my reality, through my energy offering and my intentions. Amazing news! I create my own reality. And then, I had the understanding that all is as it should be, and unwavering faith and patience is needed to let your life unfold before you. How do both exist simultaneously? How do I create my reality and simultaneously surrender to the reality that is unfolding? Through years of immersion, I began to understand how both exist simultaneously, and are in fact, one and the same. If I told you that you live for all eternity, would you ever be in a hurry? No, because you'd know that everything has enough space and time to come to life. You would be patient, you would savour the experience. Well you are eternal. The eternal infinite part of us is never in a hurry. We will experience all of it. And in fact, we already have. And simultaneously, we know that all our desires (intended and projected physical realisations) are available for realisation night now. Everything already exists as energy and is within the Quantum Field (that we are also a part of), and so everything we "want" we can have as soon as we eliminate our resistance to its realisation. The time delay (although serving), is proportionate to the depth of your resistance to said desire. So the sweet spot is knowing that there is no hurry, and all will unfold in Divine Timing (when my higher self/soul has decided it is most serving for the highest good), being in alignment (with the Universe) letting my intuitive guidance lead the way, and knowing that all that I desire, I can have here and now as soon as I realise that it was there all along. So why do we call upon (or allow) unpleasant experiences even when we are in "alignment". Because the soul knows what it needs for intentional expansion, and the expansion comes from the contrast that births the desire. And so, often the soul chooses to experience the contrast, the patterns that lead to our desire to shift, plant seeds of desire, move through and expand (into more of ourselves). The human narrative is linear in thinking, and we cannot fully comprehend the complexity (and yet simplicity) of consciousness. It is all-knowing, and time is not linear, and so it already knows all that is. Who will come in and out of your life, when we will transition from this form to the next, what lessons need to be experienced in this time and space to serve as the catalyst for expansion, and what (physical) realisations will be most serving. Our job is to surrender to it. To surrender into it, knowing that both the eternalness of our being and the conscious creator who's purpose is to expand, is operating simultaneously and is working in perfect order. If you want to go a layer deeper than that, I believe that all possibilities are happening now in parallel Universes, and so there is nothing I am not experiencing right now. But this isn't important information for the successful application of the information that preceded it.

CHAPTER 8

THE HUMAN CONDITION

There is no hurry. We shall get there someday, when the time is right, and not a moment sooner. We want everything all at once, but almost always if we were to receive it all at once we wouldn't be able to handle it. Ask for it to come in bite size pieces with ease so that it feels like the natural logical next step. I want to ease into my desires. Be crystal clear, intend, practice gratitude, take inspired action and be patient (with full embodiment of faith). All is well.

We are all related to each other. "There is but one life moving through infinite forms." I am you. You are me. I am not God, but God is me.

EIRINI

I know that our souls choose other souls to journey with in this physical realm. My sister is definitely one of my soul mates. And those who we chose allow us to grow in this physical world. There is no one in the world that triggers me more than my sister. But those triggers expose who I truly am and the areas in which I am resisting who I truly am. I am grateful to experience the triggers, the perfect mirror to my emotions. The same emotions that create my experience. And so, when my sister triggers me, it's an opportunity for me to look at myself, truly, deeply look at myself, and assess the reasons why something that is outside of me, had an effect on my emotions, the same emotions that only I can give power to. You see, her action or behaviour is indifferent. It doesn't hold any meaning to me personally, unless I give it meaning. Her behaviour towards me is about her. But my reaction to her behaviour is about me. And so when something she says bothers me, it bothers me because I am giving power to something outside of my body. I am seeing separation between me and her (the her that's really just me). I am seeing separation between me and me. I am seeing separation between me and my own reflection. I am divided within. My conscious thoughts aren't aligning with who I truly am - cosmic, infinite, expansive love. And that's why I am triggered, that's why I am in discord. And because I am aware, I can now consciously choose to change my reaction to one that aligns with my inner being. The me that is of God. The me that is love expressing itself. And so I know that I chose her, and she chose me. I chose her to have a mirror that I can check myself against every single day. She is a constant in my life. There is no life experience without her, because I have given her a role in this physical world. And I have never taken for granted just how grand, deep and powerful our bond is, and just how much it allows me to become more of myself. I am eight years her senior. My mum miscarried in between us and then she was told she could never have any more children as she would only menstruate once a year. My sister was a miracle baby. She wanted to experience this world as my parents' daughter, and as my sister. And so it is. And her name Eirini means "Peace" in Greek. And as I see my reflection through her, that is what I feel, a sense of peace. Calmness, wholeness, oneness. It isn't all triggers and growth. It is also fun, mindfulness, perfect moments, laughter, adventures, thrills, forgetting what time it is, day it is, month it is. It's everything I imagine my soul would've wanted from this human experience. It's freedom in the form of another human. I've always believed that there isn't anyone in the world like your sister. Now of course when I say that, I am referring to my own experience and perception of my world. She is someone I can share the most intimate details with, be completely myself with, never be afraid of who I am, how I am and what I desire of life. She has taught me that this deep, powerful, unconditional loving relationship exists, and if it exists with her, it can exist with everyone else on the planet too. She has taught me patience, kindness, forgiveness, love. And I too, wish that you have relationships and connections this deep, this cosmic, this enriching, because you are worthy of them. And you don't need to go looking for them, you just need to allow them in. They are all around you, and the moment you surrender and realise that the most important relationship you'll ever have is the one with yourself, then everyone else becomes a true reflection of that. They all become the best parts of you. They all become loving, deep, intimate, passionate, cosmic and wonderful, because you are first building that for yourself with yourself. You are the key. You are the key to all the relationships that you'll ever have. And we are all just extensions of each other. My neighbour is also my sister, the stranger I pass at the grocery store, is also my sister, you reading this right now, YOU are also me. I flow through you as you flow through me. We give meaning to these words. What do you want them to mean for you? I cannot control your experience, and I would never intend to, but I can show you my way, and as you cast a light on my path, you may be guided. What you perceive of me, you are perceiving of yourself. This entire book is a reflection of YOU. The you that truly deeply wants all of life. And so the next time you are triggered by anyone, take a moment to reflect how that trigger is actually discord within you. Awakening and growth are deeply personal, it's never about anyone else, it's always about us. This world does not exist without your perception of it. And the world that you perceive will never be my world, it will always be yours. And that's how you realise that you have all the power to create it as you please. What experience do you desire? How do you want your world to look? When you want your reflection to look and feel a certain way, you work on you. So I ask that you work on you. However you want to feel in the world, feel it first in your body, in your mind, in your beliefs. It's in our own vibration that we can energetically align harmoniously with well-being, love and joy.

-

I used to preach the idea of the "hustle". Until I learnt more about my connection to the Divine. Now I know it's all in the alignment. And you may even mistake that success you have from the "hustle" as real, but in fact it came from your alignment (even if you aren't consciously aware). Now don't mistake alignment for lack of effort/work, because it's all work, it's just work that starts on the inside. But you have to do the work on the outside too, but you are led intuitively through your alignment. It's easy to hustle, much harder to align.

Everything is energy. Money, love, things, people, experiences, even the air in between. It's all just energy. And you don't earn energy - actually you can't. You just need to be a conductor of it, to create a conducive environment in which you can allow the energy to flow through you. Stop resisting the flow. There is nothing more required of you than being. This human experience, this human condition is your ticket to self-worth, nothing more. Because in our essence we are from the Divine, our own Divinity is enough. What's actually required of you is less. Less resisting. Less self-sabotage. Less limitations. Less worry. Less doubt. Through this process of shedding (surrendering to your own Divinity), you will begin to welcome the flow freely. The flow of energy that is a perfect energetic match to your own frequency, the frequency of the real you - the you that comes from love, is an expression of love and will return to love. So in your pursuit of everything you've ever desired and will ever desire, remember to embrace your human condition, because it is in this human condition that we are able to desire, create and expand, it is in our own human condition that we can come to the realisation of who we truly are and remember that the Divine part of us, lives within us, and to access its infinite power, is to tune into its frequency. And you do this by aligning yourself with people, things and experiences that make you feel good. And once you do that, and enjoy the experience of it, you allow more of it to flow through you (you have now created the perfect environment in which more of the same can flow through you).

REFLECTION

Like the waves in the ocean, we ebb and flow through life. Sometimes we show up in the most exceptional way. We allow the world and other people to observe our flow. We bloom and flourish in our own poetic chaos. We overflow with love, with substance with life. We give to life more than life could ever give to us. And sometimes we show up to ourselves, to the world we retreat. But we show up to ourselves with love, with kindness, with gentleness. We fill up, we recharge. You see, we are cyclical creatures, and just as we follow moon cycles, sun cycles and earth cycles, our life is too a series of cycles. Old lessons come back to teach us something new, old wounds reopen to teach us how to heal once more. Both the ebb and the flow are just as profound, and just as important. Like the waves in the ocean, we must allow ourselves to fill up the cracks and carpet the world with love. As well as to retreat, to allow the world to give to us, to fill us up, to refuel. One is not of greater importance than the other. Actually, the only exist because of each other. Honour how you feel, honour the ebb and honour the flow. Honour where you are in the midst of the ebb and flow. Eckhart Tolle says, *"accept then act, whatever the present moment contains, accept it as if you had chosen it, always work with it, not against it. Happiness is not somewhere else, it is where you are".*

You don't become your body, your body becomes you. Once you submit to your own path of enlightenment, you begin to realise that everything is one of two things; either in alignment with who you really are (love, source, cosmic energy, infinite, everything, all), or resisting alignment.

Faith without fear is alignment, and alignment will always bring you everything you desire. Because it's when we are in alignment that we are in vibrational harmony with the energetic part of us that already has and is all things. You see, the desire itself is born *of* you, it comes from source - we are merely the vessels painting our way through this physical world - but the ideas are born from the infinite cosmos that we are - that we ALL are. So any desire that lives within you, means it is already so energetically - it isn't just possible, it is. And your job is to come to the realisation of it, and that involves alignment with it, which involves trust, unwavering faith, belief that it is already so and KNOWING. Knowing that it isn't just possible, probable or expected, but it is in fact already you, and when we know, we don't doubt or fear, because our vibrational offering is in harmony with it because we are certain, just as certain as you are that your hands are your hands. And now your body, your world and your reality will become you (the you that already exists energetically) physically.

THE HUMAN CONDITION

We are the creators and simultaneously of the creator.

-

Let's talk about true resonance.

Often when I write posts, I just allow my consciousness to flow through me and share whatever message I am called to share in the moment. Sometimes it's about abundance, love, joy, happiness, and other times it's about surrender, discomfort, pain, suffering. And more often than not I find that more people resonate with the latter. And that saddens me deeply. Because although we are here to have this human experience and attached to this experience are ALL the feelings, we are innately love, and the only feeling that should feel familiar is that of love. Everything else is foreign, feelings we learn, and they feel uncomfortable because they are not in alignment with our true spirit.

But the reason so many of us find resonance in the pain is because we allow ourselves to sit within it for too long. We neglect our personal responsibility to choose happiness, to choose to see love in all things, people and moments. The truth, is that it exists in all those things. God is omnipresent; and that truth can completely alter every single human experience you ever have, coming from a place of knowing that God always exists in every moment. And sometimes our human perception suggests that a moment isn't perfect or Divine, or that we need to ask God to come and help us over here, but God is already there, there is love there for you.

An activity I like to do with my clients, a little unconventional, but it always serves to expand consciousness, is that of exploring the "worst case scenario", tell me what it is that scares you the most about a feeling/experience/event/person. Once you say it out loud, you come to realise that even the worst possible outcome (from your human perspective) doesn't really deserve the power you give to it. We are intentionally collapsing it, it doesn't hold as much force when we consciously observe it.

Death? That is the natural process, we come from love and to love we shall return, there is nothing to fear about that.

Pain? Pain feels real, but it serves us, it lets our body know that there is work to do on healing (or better described as realising that we are resisting well-being), it lets us know that we have something more to learn about our sacred vessels and the spirit that lives within it. It allows us to observe any disharmony that may be present between your soul and your vessel. It calls for surrender, for light, for love, for understanding, for compassion, for forgiveness. God exists within it. And in the midst of the experience, often it's hard to see it that way, but that's what this work is, it's seeing beyond the veil, and coming from a place of knowing. Transcending the physical condition while also living in it.

Not many are able to handle this truth. And so they live in the discomfort, because the false familiarity of the discomfort is at least a feeling that they can predict. They can predetermine the outcome because they have played it out hundreds of times before.

I'm not here to teach you, I'm here to help you remember. We are always receiving waves and waves (and sometimes even floods and floods) of information from source. But we have to be receptive to the messages, we have to vibrate at the frequency of the language being translated through us.

I've been blessed with an innate knowing. Since I was a child. I didn't know that there was an entire spiritual community, I didn't know about metaphysics, quantum physics, consciousness, energy, vibration. I just knew what came through me. I was around 8 years old when I wrote a letter to my dad (that he was to receive in the future) that says, "I have magical powers like you". That's because that was the only way I knew how to describe it. I just knew that I could make things happen and that there was a force supporting me and guiding me at all times. I had a woman who lived in my brain, her name was "Middle-Fire" (interesting in retrospect, because really it was just a ball of light), she would talk to me everyday and share the secrets of the world with me. And as a child, this all felt safe to me, it felt like "normal".

Not many would be able to handle the imprints of information that have been brought to my conscious awareness. The infinity of it all. But one thing that I've always known is that it isn't important that we know everything, because that wouldn't serve any of us. Each of us, if we allow it, receive exactly what we need to transcend, to take a journey deeper into ourselves. And isn't that the most poetic thing you've ever heard?! Can you now understand why your soul signed up for this experience? For the unraveling of it all...

There is deep love here for you, always. But there is love everywhere for you too.

-

This came to me in a meditation. Don't analyse the validity or proof in what I'm saying, and instead revel in the beauty of revelations that come to us when we silence our thoughts and allow our higher self to talk to us. It doesn't matter if this is true or not. What matters here is that there will always be an opportunity to expand our minds, and stretch our belief system to new heights. The same way people have imagined movies about aliens, dinosaurs and fairies, we too can imagine the unimaginable, just by allowing our minds to go to those new places. Do I believe this is true? Yes. But as mentioned many times in this book, my truth does not need to align with your truth, but I will honour your truth as you honour mine. There was a time in which we co-existed with the mystical beings. Humans were both in the 3rd and 4th dimensional planes. Being both 3rd and 4th dimensional beings we were able to observe the 4th dimensional creatures. So we could see the fairies, the mermaids, the unicorns, the elves, and all the other mystical beings. That's why we have so many stories about them. That's why we can describe them with so much detail, because we lived in their world and they lived in ours. They still exist, we just aren't tuned into their frequency anymore. Although there are many accounts of people seeing them (those who cross into the 4th dimension are more receptive to them). There is a whole world we cannot physically observe. And yet it is there as a vibrational frequency. As kids we are much more likely to have the ability to see mystical beings, because we are more opened to the idea of it. The channel is open, and so the message is revealed. We allow ourselves to tune into the frequency. How can this serve us now? Imagine for a minute, what the world would look like if it were all true. Santa Clause, the Easter Bunny, fairies, ogres, avatars, werewolves, vampires, dragons, gnomes, mutants, nymphs, sirens (I was one in a past life). What would life be like? How would you see the world differently? When we allow our conscious mind to expand with possibilities, we allow room for things to come to fruition in new and unimagined ways, ways that we never believed possible. Expansion is the design. We want to stretch what's possible. As soon as it's imagined, it is made real by virtue of vibrational frequency. So strictly just science speaking here, thinking of a fairy, makes it real. And so it has the possibility to be realised. If it's possible, it's probable. It has a mathematical probability (did I mention that I used to teach Business Statistics and Business Analytics?!). Imagination is a tool. We can use this tool to create.

PRAYER

Divine Guidance, I call upon you to witness my unbecoming. Unbecoming my conditions, limits and seeming errors, and remembering my Divinity and the Source of that which I am, which is love. I ask for your hand moving forward, guide me to my path and let me feel the legions upon legions of support that comes from the spirit world. I am grateful for all the ways in which you show up for me now, I know everything is of you, but when I recognise the feathers, numbers, people, totems, I feel an immense sense of Divine Guidance. Thank you. I love you. Amen.

-

GOD IS ME

The spiritual part of us is never in a hurry because it knows that time isn't linear. The eternalness of our being means that everything unfolds in Divine timing as it should be. When we remember this truth, we are able to live life as it is. Without conditional fear that things should be other than they are. Where we are today, is exactly where we are supposed to be.

We use misdirected timelines to impose linear schedules to our lives, when really there are things that are unfolding in my life right now that were planted as seeds lifetimes and lifetimes ago. I could never plan for that using a linear calendar, there's no way I could possibly anticipate so much of the unfolding. So instead, I always wait for whatever comes, knowing that Divinity exists in all people, places, moments and experiences. But I don't discount goals and plans; because I acknowledge our Divine power to consciously create, but the intuitive nudges which lead to my intuitive actions come from a Divine place. So the timelines, the human part of me imposes, come from a limited view. Because my higher self knows when the timing is best. I will ALWAYS get what I am a vibrational match for, but I remember that it will happen when it will be most serving.

-

How do you silence the noise in an over-saturated world of information, and tune into your intuition? The world is noisy, and by that I mean that each of us think around 60,000 - 80,000 thoughts a day, and many of those thoughts we share with others. Those thoughts are mostly unconscious thoughts, we don't intentionally plant them, we instead think by default, based on what our subconscious beliefs are, our lifetime of conditioning, our perception of reality, our level of understanding and interpreting stimuli and how we feel emotionally in the moment. I've recently been reading the book E-Squared by Pam Grout. A great read for those who tend to find "spiritual" books too complex, or need a simplified approach to understanding the laws of the Universe. She provides 9 experiments which "prove" that the Universe is always working with us. In one chapter she makes reference to the Conscious mind as serving two purposes; to recognise contrast (something that doesn't align), and then to plant the seed (of desire to something that IS aligned), then we should revert back to our intuitive guidance. But instead, us humans tend to let our conscious minds take the wheel and have way too much control over the direction we are moving. We let our minds think about the pros, cons, the possibilities, the things that could go wrong, the reasons why it won't happen, we even use our past as evidence that it hasn't worked before, so why should it be any different this time around. But by letting our conscious mind take the wheel, we are denying ourselves the opportunity to tap into our higher self, the self that is at the peak of the mountain, who can foresee all that is to be, because it already is. The conscious mind allows for conscious creation and expansion - we signed up for this, it's what we want, BUT we knew coming here that we would ALWAYS be tapped into the part of us that is all-knowing, that knows the path that is for the highest good, that knows the next step. Our ancestors lived off this knowing, but along the way, we were confined, told to follow predetermined structures and rules that suppressed our connection to the Divine. And for most of us, it is like a forgotten memory that sometimes creeps through, when we are relaxed enough, but we overlook it as just our imagination playing wild games like an untamed cub in the jungle. We mask our natural guidance system because we have been conditioned to believe that our rational mind should supersede all other "minds". But this is the moment, that your awareness of your Divinity has been remembered, and just as you wouldn't want a high school student who dreams of becoming a surgeon to perform surgery on you, why are we giving something that does not have the credentials the driver's seat. Let's give the role back to the professional. Let's remember that we are here to observe the contrast, then to plant the seed, then to revert back to our decision-making professional, which will never lead us astray. And this process doesn't have to look like deep meditation every time we want guidance. For me it's as simple as asking, "What would God say to me about this?" - the all-knowing, unlimited, every possibility is probable God, say to me. And when my ego wants to resist the answer, I KNOW that it's the right one - because the conscious mind will try and jump in there and bring me back to "safety" (the ego likes to keep us "safe" in the bubble of the unknown, even the uncomfortable unknown, because it's discomfort that is predictable because we've lived it on repeat for so long, or at least been exposed to the predictable discomfort for so long).

-

PRAYER

Divine Guidance, I pray that all is well. I pray that I have an innate knowing that everything is always well and that I remember that my perception will always be limited because of my human condition - but that I am simultaneously of you, therefore the part of me that is spirit, the part of me that offers no resistance, will always guide me. And my job is to surrender and listen to the intuitive guidance and maintain my alignment with it. I hear you. Thank You. I love you. And so it is. Amen.

CHAPTER 9

YOU ARE THE DREAMER OF YOUR DREAM

Every single moment is the perfect moment and enough. And the only moment that I ever need to focus fully on is this one. And the goal of each moment is joy. And if in this moment I feel anything other than that of joy, I have <u>complete</u> control over what I choose to feel in the next moment and that's because my power of creation is right now. And my vibrational frequency and consequently the vibration that I am attracting is that of which I am transmuting (offering) right now - because it is now in which I hold all my power. But your choice is in your focus. There is no "yes" or "no", there is only "yes" and the yes responds to your focus. So what I focus on now is what I'm choosing for next. In order to intentionally create all I have to do is focus on the thoughts and feelings I desire and feel my way through the flow. That is to use my feelings and emotions to let me know how close or how far away I am from who I truly am. The better I feel, the closer I am. And your feelings do not need to be dependent on anything outside of you, because it's with your thoughts and your perception of those thoughts that you determine how you feel.

If you can't change the way you feel about something, change your focus instead, choose to focus on something that you already know makes you feel good. That will, intentionally and consequently, raise your vibrational frequency. This game of life isn't designed to be hard, it's designed to be fun, light and playful. Have fun, wake up and decide how you wish to feel that day, and do as many things as you can during your day to bring on the feeling you intended for. I can spill my tea and be mad, or I can spill my tea and laugh hysterically. I get to decide. I'm generally a clumsy person, whether it's some imbedded belief from my youth or not, I don't know, but regardless, at least once a day I'll spill something, drop something, rip something, or something like it, and if I got upset every time that happened, I'd be living a lot of my life angry. And that is way too heavy for me to allow into my experience. So instead I laugh about it, I say thank you for it, because it reminds me, every single day, to not take life so seriously, to allow what is, versus trying to control everything. And because I am allowing it and enjoying it, I create more to bring me joy and flow.

LETTER TO MYSELF

The words "Thank You" do not even begin to describe how I truly feel. And I know that true gratitude towards God is the embodiment and expression of love and joy, and in every possible way I try to commit to living through my immense gratitude. I am truly and deeply living my best life. I am so happy, I am so grateful. I am so loved and supported. The Divine has shown itself to me in infinite ways this year and I feel incredibly connected to source. I see myself in everyone and I love the reflections of myself that I observe. I understand more and more why I chose this time and space and this physical reality. I understand that I came to experience it all and live a full life and to allow God to work through me to spread the message of light and love. It is very clear to me that I impact millions of people in a very positive and enlightened way. I know that my mission here involves being seen and heard by millions all over the world and I celebrate and welcome the world's love into my life - joyously. I am so grateful that my creative expression shines through my mission and that I can look back and celebrate that it all came to me so easily - because I allowed it to, because I had unquestionable faith in God and the Universe to deliver, and because I asked and expected it to flow to me. My vibration sets the standard. I embody love - in all its forms. I am happy. I am loved. I am loving. I am rich. I am beautiful. I am strong. I am fit. I am inspirational. I am intelligent. I am important - integral in fact. I am grateful. I am grateful for the expansion. I am grateful that I've been able to find that deep love that I desired - and I found it through my own deep love for myself. Thank you for the richness that I now experience. I am in love with my life. I am grateful beyond words, and I will continue to express my gratitude through the embodiment of love and joy - because that's how God chooses to express Himself through me. I am embracing the continual expansion of my life. I am the person that I've always believed that I was. Thank you. I love you. Infinitely. And most of all, I am grateful for the experience of true love. God's true love for me. That is certain.

You create the world that you know. We are artists. Creating both glories and terrors. We are always in a state of becoming. We are not static.

RAMPAGE

We believe that our consciousness is linear; past, present, future... But that's not the case.

Do you want to be limited? Or do you want to be free? What if the future can appear just as clear as the past...?

YOU ARE THE DREAMER OF YOUR DREAM

Do your memories feel real?

Do you believe they happened?

Do you feel certain?

But are they happening now?

So how can we feel certain?

We are certain in our KNOWING.

And it is in our KNOWING that we create all matter.

They exist, not just because we can see them in our minds,
not just because we believe they did, but because we
KNOW without holding any resistance, that they did.

It is in this place, that we create all things, feelings and
experiences.

Our consciousness is always experiencing now. Now existed
in the past and it will exist in the future. Now is the only
moment that you will experience in this physical world. And
it's in the now that you have the power to create any emotion
that you desire. If we relive a past experience through
memory, we re-invite the emotion into the now. If we imagine
a future experience through visualisation, we pre-invite the
emotion into the now. It's always here and it's always now.

You don't get what you want, you get what you are.

Prepare vibrationally. Prepare for it. It's coming. How will you
act once it's here? Act that way now. Act as if.

Your thoughts create your reality. It takes a thought to form a word. A thought to form a belief. That belief turns into a feeling. And that feeling attracts that which is like it. The world you see is a reflection of the way you feel.

Feeling good is the work. That's how you get into alignment. Feel good first, then everything will flow to you with ease.

Don't resist well-being, welcome it.

If you can feel it, then you'll soon see it.

Repeat this after me, "I feel it and soon I'll see it, I feel it and soon I'll see it, I feel it and soon I'll see it."

Once the desire has formed as a thought and you project to the Universe your desire to live that thought, it is instantly answered and created. Your job is to now come to the realisation of it. The winning lottery ticket is in your pocket, but you aren't checking your pockets. Be thankful that it's already so, be grateful that you are living your best life, be grateful that the flow of abundance and well-being is ever-increasing in your life. Be so confident that the desire is already so, that the physical manifestation of it is no longer necessary, because you taste the juice of the fruit already.

And once you surrender in this way, it will flood to you in avalanches.

Imagine everything that is your life; your finances, your career, your mindset, your emotions, your physical body, your family, your love, your entire life. Now imagine yourself winning at all of them. Imagine the best possible version of each, and feel the feelings of fulfilment in each area.

Who are you with?
What are you doing?
How do you feel?
What does it sound like?
What does it look like?
What emotions are you experiencing?
How can it be better? What would bring complete happiness and fulfilment? And then go to that place in your mind.

You are not limited by physical conditions, in your mind you can travel to wherever you desire in a moment. You can be a Queen, an astronaut, a CEO, a mum, a lover, a writer, a traveller, whatever you desire, in just a moment. You can float between your desires in a moment. And your mind does not know the difference between what you see with your mind's eye and what you see with your physical eyes. So vibrationally, you begin to align with the reality you expose yourself to, the most often. The reality you believe. So start believing the reality of your best self, the version of you that already exists in your mind. Your physical world will have no choice but to catch up.

You are so full. You couldn't possibly imagine how full you are. But try. Try to imagine your fullness. You come from love and to love you shall return, and your journey here is an expression of love. And love is infinite, so despite how much you give, you are always still completely full. The richness you attract into your life, is OF you, it comes from you, it was never separate from you, you always had it, it was always there, you are just now coming to the realisation of it.

You don't need to wish. You just need to become.

What you think about, you become.
What you dwell on, you become.
What you embrace, you become.
What you expel, you become.
What you focus on, you become.

Repeat after me, "I am experiencing consecutive wins, healing, unexpected blessings, growth, financial freedom, spiritual insight, and infinite love."

Fear is just a manifestation of the ego.

We come from love and to love we shall return. That means that our entire experience here, in this physical world, is aligned with well-being and feeling good. So when something doesn't feel good it's because who we truly are feels discord with that feeling. It's a foreign feeling. Fear isn't a natural state of being, it's just the resistance to well-being. It's born from this world, not the spiritual world. It comes from our ego and not our true self. Fear sees separation between ourselves and our desired state, faith on the other hand, sees oneness with where I am and where I desire to be, and oneness with yourself and God. You can be happy and feel good 100% of the time, and if you don't it's because you are resisting it, not because it's not available to you.

Repeat after me, "I welcome well-being and feeling good into my life. I acknowledge that it's my natural state and I align myself with people and experiences that match that feeling."

Think of the placebo effect, when a stimulus is used in lieu of the common believed solution, and the patient consumes the stimulus and often sees significant results. The placebo is just your own beliefs. The patient believed something would work and so it did. The common belief in this world is that 2+2 is 4, but 2+2 can be whatever you want it to be. You decide what beliefs live within you, they don't have to align with the dominant narrative, and your reality becomes a projection of those beliefs.

Your beliefs determine who you are and who you are becoming. And that is the vibration that you emit to attract anything and everything that matches that frequency. So your sole purpose is to get into alignment with everything you desire. What you desire isn't physical, as it may often seem, it is instead a desired feeling. You desire to feel good, be happy, experience joy. And so to align with these desired feelings, you need to embody them now, in every way that you can. Your job is to feel good. That is the work. And then the path will reveal itself to you. In fact, revelations are always, constantly happening. But we often miss them, because we aren't in alignment. So acknowledge when you have moments of realisation. It's in those moments that you are in tune, in alignment and ready to receive the revelation.

Repeat this after me, "Feeling good is the work. Feeling good is the work, and I am embodying the feeling of joy, happiness and freedom."

Regardless of how far reaching they may seem, keep your dreams and desires alive. The law of one acknowledges that when a desire is born, with it, so is the means to fulfil that desire. We all have moments of doubt, worry, fear, but don't let those feelings, that are NOT truth, stop you from moving forward anyway, don't fixate on the perceived limitations.

It doesn't matter your age, gender, nationality, religion or current situation… you are worthy. You don't need to prove your worth. Your life is proof that you are worthy. You don't need to pray more, buy more crystals, do readings, practice yoga, to be connected to God. You can if you want to, if you're called to. But you are worthy just as you are and just as much as everyone else. So begin to act that way, act expectant, act as if, act excited, act motivated, act victorious. That's how you begin to enjoy the fruits of life.

We often become so focused on the end result that we forget to embrace the journey. And when we look back we realise that it was the journey that bared all the fruit. That doesn't mean that there isn't joy in the fulfilment of a desire, there is, of course there is, and focusing upon that end result will get you there faster. But in the mean time, come to the realisation that the journey there is part of the manifestation experience. It is the process of becoming the person who has the desire, who IS the desire.

Repeat this after me, "I'm literally in the best shape of my life; physically, emotionally, mentally, spiritually, socially and financially."

The feeling of fulfilment exists right now. You can enjoy every single day of your life to the fullest. The time between the birth of a desire and the fulfilment of it serves you, because it allows you to grow and to learn. And at times to evolve, both you and the desire may evolve. And the time lap allows you to embody the feeling before you see the physical proof of it - you trust the vibrational manifestation of it. You visualise, you see it in your minds eye, you use stimuli to feel it in this physical world the best way you can. Visualisation leads to the feeling of having it now. You feed your subconscious mind visuals, sounds, smells, tastes and feelings that train your mind to emit a frequency that matches those feelings. You will feel so good in the process and that alignment will attract inspired action - the only action that will bring forth your desires. When you feel an intuitive nudge, act on it, don't question or doubt it, just move forward, you can never get it wrong. You are always on your path and everything is always working out for you.

Repeat this after me, "I'm always on my path and everything is always working out for me."

We come from one energy field, one eternal light, and that supply is unlimited. Just as a wave is an individualisation of the ocean, your soul is an individualisation of God, of that one energy field. And so anything that comes from the source, which is everything, so too can be yours. We are unlimited beings, we have no ceiling. Your purpose is what you say it is, what you have and what you are is what you say it is. Our words are attached to our beliefs and our beliefs determine our feelings which determine our vibration, which is our point of attraction.

It really is simple. Behave like you have it, believe you have it, feel good now, follow the intuitive nudges, enjoy the journey as though it has all already happened for you, and so it will appear in physical form, because vibrationally it is already so.

When you come across feelings of resistance and disbelief, take a moment to realign. Announce, "I don't accept that negative energy, I don't accept that fear. I am love. I am positivity. Everything flows through me."

Speak those words with conviction. Repeat them again and again, until they feel like the truth. And if you still feel resistance when you speak them, then there are underlying beliefs that are not truth that you have programmed into your subconscious and your reality is a reflection of those falsehoods. And so, you need to reprogram your beliefs to align with your truth. The truth that you are worthy, that you are connected to the unlimited supply of source, that you are already full, that you are infinitely loved and guided, that all is well, that you are always on your path, that happiness is a choice and is available to you at all times.

Often people create complexities in the spiritual world because then it becomes easier to accept that it's because we aren't able to understand and apply the complex theories and laws that we aren't living our desires. But that's another falsehood that we accept. Instead, come to the realisation that this process is easy. Your life is easy. It's a complex world, but your job is to enjoy the complexities in the most joyful and easy way. Feel good. Feel good. Feel good. That will look different to each of us, and that's ok. In fact, that's the design. Your way, is the way.

My truth is my own and it does not need to align with your truth. My truth isn't THE truth, but my truth is very real to me. And my truth determines how I think, feel and perceive my reality, thus our realities will all vary because they are dependent on our own truths.

YOU ARE THE DREAMER OF YOUR DREAM

Your truth is the only truth that matters, the only truth that creates your reality.

Repeat after me, "When I honour my true self, the self that is in perfect harmony with the Universe, I open the doors and allow everything I desire to flow to me with ease."

Don't overthink this process. Your only goal right now is to feel good. To feel happy. To feel grateful for the many blessings that are constantly flowing to you. The intuitive action, the manifestations, the process of becoming, that all happens with ease and naturally. Allow it to be easy. Allow yourself to be at peace and satisfied with the way things are right now, yet simultaneously excited and expectant that more is on its way to you.

Repeat after me, "I am so happy now, everything is perfect and I am whole-heartedly grateful for the way it has manifested so far, and I am eager for more."

You don't get what you want, you get what you are.

And so it is.

PRAYER

Feeling the juice of my life brings me so much gratitude and joy. I'm filled with appreciation that I get to experience life in this way. Knowing that I am always on my path and always getting it right. Your love surrounds me and I feel you lift me, guide me and pull me closer to you. I hear the call from my soul and I always know what the next best move is, and I am trusting that call, because I know that it comes from the part of me that is you. Right now, as I am, with all I have, and with all of the love that lives within me, I feel wholeness, oneness. And nothing more is required than for me to maintain this feeling forever. I love you. And whatever you would have me do, I am willing to do my part, knowing that you are always doing yours. Forever yours. Amen.

Creation. Expansion. Joy. Playfulness. That's why we are here. This we know. Micro and macro perspective in mind. Individual and collective consciousness. I grow as one, and simultaneously grow the collective. And out of all the playful techniques and tools I've used to expand, my favourite one, and the one I started doing as a child (before I knew what The Law of Attraction was), is called THE MONOLOGUE METHOD (a name I coined myself). Similar to scripting and acting as if, but instead I rehearse a monologue. Usually in the car, as I feel it's the most conducive environment for this activity, I imagine myself on a stage, any stage, speaking to an audience of people, either being interviewed or being asked to share my story with the world. And I begin my monologue, sharing my journey, my wins, my challenges, the feelings I felt on the way, everything. The monologue is rehearsed as though I'm ALREADY living the life I envision. I'm at the other end telling my story. I love it mostly because, I don't have to lie to my conscious or subconscious mind, because I still reflect on the feelings and the reality of the present moment, the only difference is that I'm speaking from the perspective of future Gee (which if you've read this book, you know that I believe that future and past you can only be experienced right now - and so I'm giving her life right now). Let me give you an example, here's a monologue from an interview about my book just selling over 400 million copies worldwide...

"I know it's incredible right?! I remember when I would look up how many Harry Potter books had been sold around the world, because J K Rowling was a huge mentor for me, and I was so inspired by her story. And one day I saw the number 400 million, which I know the Harry Potter series has far surpassed that now, but that number just resonated with me. And it became my target. I imagined myself selling 400 million copies around the world, having the book translated into many languages and even being on TV shows just like this one sharing my story. And now I'm here. Funnily enough, I actually wrote about this experience in my book, playing out exactly like this, and as I was writing it, I could see you all, I could feel your love, I could feel my pen signing all your copies, and I knew that this book was going to change the lives of hundreds of millions of people. God chose to work through me in this way, and although there were times where I felt as though my path was cloudy, I always knew that the path would be lit regardless. I was always on my path, and you are always on yours. You can't just believe it though, because even belief holds resistance, you have to know. Because when you know, you behave like you know, you go about your day like you know, you change the way you speak and move, because you already know how it will all play out. Just like I did for this moment right here. And the truth is, that although God was working through me and I was living my purpose, and of course still am, this book was always about serving YOU. This book was bigger than I was. And I remember sharing that line with the members of a course I was enrolled in about writing a book proposal, and I received feedback that saying that the book was bigger than I was, and bigger than we all were, came across too confident and that I should reword it, and it was then that I realised just how important this book was, and that we were so used to being conditioned that most of us had forgotten who we were. And I am so honoured that I have been able to share this collection of reflections with you, and I know that you will each receive exactly what you need from this book, and you will come back to it forever, always finding something new. I want you to know that I am so incredibly grateful to be sitting here sharing my story with you all and I thank you deeply for following your intuition and buying my book. The grandness of that I will never take for granted. I love you all so deeply, and thank you for having me on the show."

Can you see the power in that monologue?! The magnitude of the vibrational offering that I'm projecting when I say that out loud in my car, rehearsing it from my heart?!

I never say the same monologue twice, I rehearse them as though I'm being interviewed many many times and each time I bring something new to the table. You can apply the monologue method to any desire, feeling or experience. I change between my desires. Sometimes talking about my house, sometimes my book, sometimes my business, anything and everything. It brings me joy, I never take it too seriously and I always have fun with it.

VISUALISE

Similarly to the Monologue Method, I use a process called a Vision Statement to program my subconscious mind into pre-living my future as though it were a past memory. Time is not linear, and just as easily as I can access my past memories, I can access my future memories. This process allows me to create from the Quantum Field; condensing time and space in the 3 Dimensional world, because I'm creating from the 5 Dimensional world.

This process was inspired by Yahya Bakkar. When I read his Vision Statement, I felt a deep resonance with this process. I am about to share mine with all of you. It is sacred to me. I allow it to evolve if it needs to. But something I feel I need to share with you all, is that I resonate more with the person described in my statement than the person who wrote it. I have become the version of me that I remembered I already was.

You create your Vision Statement by writing out your perfect day, in past tense, as though you have already experienced it and you are just rewriting it out in your journal. I recommend that the first time you do this, you hand write it, this helps with the programming. After that, you can type it up and read it to yourself everyday. Be mindful of who you choose to share it with. What you focus on expands. What you allow others to focus on with you, expands 100-fold. And if others aren't at a place on their journey that they can understand these concepts, they may be focusing on the "falsehood" of this approach, thus expanding a vibrational frequency of doubt. I share mine with you, because if you've made it this far into the book, you are definitely on board, and I know that as I expand, you expand with me, we expand the collective, we become more of ourselves, we become more love.

So here it is:

Grigoria Kritsotelis

My Vision. My Life. My Creation. My Expansion.

Written on 27 June 2018

GOD IS ME

My perfect day begins like this...

It was absolutely incredible. I am so grateful and full of appreciation that I could experience a day so perfect. I woke up naturally - no alarms, to the beautiful sound of the waves of the Australian ocean dancing with each other, the soft wind as the music, and I felt so peaceful and calm, and so connected to the parts of me who lived with them. And then the sun kissing my skin through the window and gently teasing me to wake up. I sat up, thanked you for your grace, stretched and listed all the things I'm grateful for. Watching the ocean fills me with so much joy. It felt incredible to look through all my bedroom windows and watch the ocean. The sun was shining through my window and I felt her heat on my skin. I was fully present in the moment, appreciating her loving warmth.

As I rose, I went to the kitchen to prepare a warm water with lemon and ginger. I sat in my day bed overlooking the ocean, enjoying the view, wearing my silky nighty, which always makes me feel sexy and feminine, Goddess-like. I live in the most incredible house; my dream house. The house I've always envisioned. Two story, open-living, beautiful coastal barn style, white and neutral colour palette, the perfect house.

I walk into my room and get dressed into my gym clothes. I sprayed my favourite perfume, put on my essential oils, brushed my teeth and washed my face, and made my way into my yoga room. I completed a 20 minute yoga flow with the most beautiful rainforest soundtrack in the background, overlooking my beautiful garden. I thanked my Divine body for being such a gracious and powerful vessel. When I finished I made my way, fully energised and invigorated, to my gym room. I started with a 10 minute cardio warmup, followed by an intense lower body weighted session. I love having a gym at home - it makes my life so much easier and I'm so grateful. I love moving my vessel and I love my body. It's healthy, full of vitality and I'm sexy AF! Perfect flat stomach, defined abs, peachy booty, toned legs and arms and the most beautiful skin and hair. I'm literally in the best shape of my life; physically, emotionally, mentally, spiritually, socially and financially.

After my incredible workout, I make my way into my sauna. I spent 20 minutes in the sauna, I love the heat and the way it makes me sweat. I played music while enjoying the sauna. Post sauna, I was ready to shower, I went into my ensuite and had a warm shower, perfect water pressure, perfect temperature, and with my diffuser on in the background and the perfect ylang ylang smell in the air - I was in heaven. Best shower, I love my ensuite, I put my deodorant on, moisturised my body and my face with my mums world famous organic skincare range, put perfume on, rubbed on my essential oils and got dressed into the perfect outfit - black jeans, a flowy black top, sandals and a long cardigan.

I decide to make my way to the market to buy some fresh produce. The weather was perfect, so I hop into my white Porsche 4wd and drive to the market. In my basket I collect the most beautiful array of colourful fruits and vegetables along with some buckwheat pasta, kombucha, kimchi, nuts and raw treats. I also pick up a beautiful bunch of white flowers filled with greenery for my kitchen.

I'm surrounded by kind people and I love the beautiful cosmic energy surrounding me. I make my way home, unpack and make myself a warm bowl of peanut butter turmeric oats, a protein smoothie and a peppermint tea. Admiring my flowers as I enjoyed my first meal.

It was then time to get into alignment and start my "work" day - which felt much more like "play" day (as it always does). I walk into my stunning white office, that overlooks the ocean and sit at my grand desk and write my gratitude list; I'm thankful for so much, everything in fact, I cry sometimes in awe of how incredibly aligned I feel, God is good and life is filled with blessings. I meditate; my favourite daily practice by far, it always raises my vibration and gets me into alignment real quick. I journal; this time I journaled about my life around the world, and the fact that I had beautiful homes in all my favourite places in the world.

One in Bali, overlooking the ocean, an outdoor bathroom, beautiful villa, we spend a lot of time in Bali and I love it so much, it's such a sacred, sunny and spiritual place, one in Greece, on an island, my motherland, I always feel at home in Greece, speaking the language fluently is a bonus, and now we are planning on finding our next home in the world. I listen to a video and reach a high vibration and I check my emails. The first email was from my book agent and publisher, I had a $200,000 day yesterday with online sales, so without trading my time for money. This is happening DAILY! Bliss. Life is beautiful. I created my life. I created this ease and flow. I felt the feelings of having it all long before I did. Whatever I desire and imagine for myself, I create, instantly. Because I believe it to be so. Health, wealth, love, success, whatever it is, it's already mine. I felt so incredibly grateful and blessed that I make money so easily through my writing. I received a few more emails with confirmations for paid speaking gigs, new students signing up to my various online courses overnight (amounting to thousands of dollars overnight), new guests signing up to my many retreats, sales from mum's skincare and dad's art, so many beautiful emails from clients and strangers admiring my work, an email confirming my meeting with one of the most recognised talk show hosts in the world, people crediting me for inspiring them, guiding them and changing their lives and an email from YouTube telling me I've just surpassed 1 MILLION subscribers! I share a few posts with my current Soul Food students, then communicate with my team to prepare for my upcoming launch of Inception. I thought to myself, "How is this my life?!" We already had 44 students sign up to Inception before any marketing - so over $20,000 with ease flowed to me. I recorded a few videos for YouTube in my office. I love inspiring people to become more connected to their true selves. I want everyone to grow and come to the realisation of who they truly are - pure, cosmic love. We are all one with the Divine, and although I may not be God, God is me. And the more often I spread that message, the further the ripple flows. I am a light worker. I embody life every single day. I continue living my best life. I decide to book an impromptu trip to Morocco for my husband and I, just to celebrate life, continue being youthful and adventurous. I also started planning a VIP event that I will host in my home, inviting the most inspiring light workers from all over the world. Because I'm known as one of the top spiritual teachers and mindset coaches in the world, I have celebrities, leaders, speakers, coaches, entrepreneurs, game-changers, and other influencers consult and collaborate with me on a regular basis to guide them to their own inner guidance system to uncover and become more of themselves in the most poetic, light-filled way. I have a social network that impacts millions of people, and that's because I am always Grigoria. The Divine, always connected to her soul, leading the way by light, Grigoria. I'm making multiple 8 figures a year living a luxurious, attractive, abundant and authentic lifestyle that's true to my deepest desires. I work with people so that they can remember what their souls have always known - that they are pure love, and that love is not faulted, and that love can be, do and have all things. You are worthy just because you are.

I then decided I was done playing in the office. I made my way to my library and spent 30 minutes reading, the sun peeping through the window, warming my cheek. I spent a moment admiring my beautiful art pieces and sculptures. It was then time to cook dinner, I was having Eirini and friends over. And just as I start cooking, my sexy, smart, funny, handsome, woke husband arrives home. "Hey baby" he says as he planted a big, juicy, bold kiss on my lips. I love our relationship so much, we continue falling deeper in love and more and more cosmically soul connected.

I went and got dressed into a pretty black dress, I spent a moment to appreciate and admire how incredibly beautiful I looked. Perfect abs, perfect face, so pretty, so full of vitality. Hair looked like a Goddess.

My kitchen is my haven. I made my famous buckwheat pasta with creamy pasta sauce, salad and steamed veggies. Served with kombucha and wine. My sister and friends arrived, I had my candles burning, I had saged the house, incense burning and my diffuser on. We sat around my big table outside on the deck and enjoyed our fabulous dinner - jazz, soul and a little old school RnB playing in the background. After dinner, some of my guests had a swim in the pool, I enjoyed the beach view and laughed with my friends, sister and husband. For dessert I had prepared a raspberry vegan cheesecake the day before. We all loved it and enjoyed the company. All my food made with love and eaten in love is pure, divine, cosmic energy and will nourish every cell in my body, and I always feel elated from eating food. It makes me youthful.

My guests started to leave, but they all helped clean up first. Eirini was staying in the guest house with her boyfriend, so we said our goodnights.

My husband and I sat in the lounge, snuggled and watched a romantic movie. Then we made our way to bed where we had incredible passionate sex and fell asleep watching the ocean waves and stars reflection.

YOU ARE THE DREAMER OF YOUR DREAM

It was the perfect day. Thank you God. It is a perfect life. And tomorrow my parents are coming for dinner, art chats, scotch and cigars.

I get to be me, and be everyone and everything. The magnitude of that I never take for granted.

I, Grigoria Kritsotelis, promise to stay true to my vision and values no matter what. If I ever lose confidence in myself, doubt or start to fear, I will reread this document to remind me of how powerful and valuable I truly am, and how important it is for me to always be my true self, the self that I am vibrationally.

I love you big G (God) <3

Grigoria Kritsotelis

My Core Values:

Love . Alignment . Freedom . Health . Wealth . Growth .

Expansion . Energy . Passion . Joy . Happiness .

Wholeness . Oneness . Light . Courage . Humility .

Inspiration . Fun . Charisma . Enlightenment .

Empowerment . Contribution . Trust . Authenticity .

Abundance . Awareness . Self-Awareness . Success

CHAPTER 10

THE RESURRECTION

So let's say that the words written here held some sort of meaning to you, some new perspective of your reality... Now what? How do you use it?

A belief is a thought you keep thinking. And at any point you have the power to change your thought patterns and alter your beliefs, which in turn alter your feelings, which alter your vibrational frequency, which alter your physical manifestations (i.e the reality you perceive). So decide now what it is you want to experience, and change your thought patterns, beliefs and feelings to match that desired experience. Remember time is not linear. What you want to experience *then*, you can experience *now*, through your focus on it. Through your embodiment of it. Through the reflection of it. God is me. God is you. God is all of us. And just as God has the power to create anything at anytime, you too hold the power to do so. Ask, receive, believe. The life experience you desire is not over there, it never has been, it's been here all along, and it always will be. You are the leader, the creator.

You may be a creator, but know that you are simultaneously experiencing this world through you. Life is by you, but also for you. You have the ability to channel life, embody the frequency of this world, as well as the world you came from, the world of love. You get to surrender, you don't need to move so fast, yield to it, surrender to it. And in time you will come to realise your wholeness, your oneness with God and with all. You are the wave, the tree, the air, the friend, you are all of it, you are here experiencing yourself. The profoundness of that may seem like a lot, but your soul gets it, the deeper part of you understands. And wherever you are right now on your spiritual journey, be all there, and allow it to be what it is. Don't judge it, experience it, learn from it, let it work through you, from you, as you.

You've heard me say the before, but just as a wave is an individualisation of the ocean, and as one wave moves, the entire ocean moves. We are individualisations of God. And as each one of us moves, evolves and expands, so does the collective. You are both an atom and a wave, both static and moving. Each wave is significant, important and necessary. Each one of us is significant, important and necessary.

THE RESURRECTION

This book wasn't designed to inspire, although that may be a by-product, it was designed to awaken. Awaken the God that lives within you. Whether you believe it or not, God is you. Some may never discover their own innate power, and others will harness it to consciously create the life experience they desire. Ultimately it's up to you, which you are. Reaching this far in the book suggests to me that you are the latter. You are here to consciously create, to joyously expand, to remember. And I commend you. I commend you for listening to the intuitive nudges that led you here, the intuitive nudges that guide you. Those intuitive nudges come from your inner being, the inner being that is of God. And so the next time you see separation between you and anyone, you and anything, you and any feeling, remind yourself of this moment, the moment that you consciously made the realisation that God is you and anything that comes from God, comes from you, and you have access to the Divine infinite power of God anytime you choose to call upon it. Believe it so deep in your soul that anything that doesn't align with that truth, is false. That anything that doesn't confirm your Divinity, isn't real.

-

What is it to channel? What is it to allow God to answer prayers through you? What is it to realise your Divinity through your Divine expression? To channel is to allow God to speak through you. And often it's less about words and more about the feelings attached to the inspired thoughts that flow to you.

This is how I channel. Firstly, I need to be completely "tapped in"; I need to surrender my conscious thoughts, I need to let my mind drift to a place that is beyond this time and space reality, I need to completely surrender to the experience, and I need to allow whatever comes through to have a moment on the stage if it wants it. This is best achieved through meditation. Any form of meditation, but often for me it involves sound frequency (528 hz or 432 hz are my frequencies of choice). After meditation, I come back to my conscious state with a host of revelations. Some that I understand, and others that I can't interpret in that moment. Before meditating, I always command that not only can I receive messages that I will be able to interpret, but that I can also translate those messages in a way that others can receive fully. And here I am, having just done a channelling session, being told that before I channel anything more for this book, I need to explain to you what the process looks and feels like. I often say that prayer is praying (talking to) the part of you that offers no resistance, and that's why it is so powerful. That is the same with channelling. It is asking the part of you that is the collective, for the guidance, answers, revelations. It offers no resistance, it is all knowing. Every thought ever thought exists within it. There is nothing that has been revealed that isn't accessible to you. And that doesn't just include human consciousness, that includes all beings (whether you believe in them or not).

Think of carbon imprints. When you copy something, the carbon copy remains in the collective, so all things physically realised, first came from the Source. They existed as non-physical energy before they became physical. And many things never become physical, they just exist as energy in the collective consciousness. Your past life memories exist in that same consciousness, your future life memories and thoughts exist in that same consciousness too. As do the parallel universes, different dimensions and infinite timelines. Because as we have discussed, time is not linear, and the best way to understand it is to ask yourself where a circle begins and ends. That is how time, or at least our understanding of it, works too.

I know that there are some of you reading this now that question the validity of these words. You ask for the science, the proof, the evidence, the studies, and all the things you think you need to form or reform a belief. But you won't find that in this body of work. This work is an intuitive understanding of my Divine expression. I don't need to prove any of these reflections to myself, as they feel like truth to me. And they allow me to understand my own truth as I navigate through this physical experience. So with that I avoid the need to prove it to you too. What resonates and feels like truth may become your truth too, and what doesn't will fall away from your conscious awareness anyway. But all of this remains in the collective consciousness for anyone and everyone to access for infinity.

-

As you may have observed from this book, I channel most in two instances; when I speak and when I meditate. This beautifully channeled piece came to me during meditation, but was confirmed when someone asked me a question about it and this is what I blurted out... I was asked, if the same number of souls always exist. Because we often refer to the collective consciousness, where all souls exist. So the question is valid. And for a long time I couldn't answer it. Until one day, I was given a moving picture of bacteria and it all made sense. Imagine looking under a microscope and watching bacteria split into two, four, sixteen new cells. Then imagine also observing multiple cells, turn back into one cell. That's what our souls are like. There is ONE energy for which we all come from, but there are not a finite number of souls. We split, we merge, we remain, depending on what we need on our journeys, what we need for expansion. Sometimes the same soul travels though lifetimes upon lifetimes, and sometimes that soul splits into two searching for itself again in each lifetime (think twin flames), and sometimes two souls become one (think about twins, who may come back as one person in the next life), and most times, each soul is comprised of many souls (because they are all in the collective pool until needed to journey back here). When I call upon my deceased grandfather, his resonance can feel me. Like a carbon copy. But do I believe he is still my grandfather as one soul? No. He goes back into the pool of souls. He may come back again, or he may become two people, or part of him may merge with another part and become someone new. This may all seem strange, and unfamiliar. But tonight as you wander off to sleep, I want you to ask God for a revelation during your slumber, and see what is revealed through your dreams. This concept was not ever a conscious thought for me before it was revealed to me during meditation. I could not have imagined that this is how it worked. And yet now I believe it with complete certainty.

-

GOD IS ME

CALLING UPON YOU

I call upon you. I call upon you to witness yourself rise. I call upon you to feel the magnitude of cosmic love and support that exists for you. I call upon you to release any and all misguided beliefs, perceived pain and seeming errors. Let God take anything that no longer serves you so that you can be reminded of the love that you have been resisting. I call upon you to step into your role. Your desire to be has to match your willingness to be. Rise. You are Divinely supported. I call upon you to realise and receive your blessings. You may not understand how you're being blessed, but know that you are. I call upon you to remember that you come from love and to love you shall return and your journey and purpose here is to be an expression of that love. I call upon you to share, to serve, to love and to awaken. And may the abundance that you are flood to every aspect of your life. And so it is.

PRAYER

Divine Guidance, I call upon youth show me the path of light so that I can serve at my fullest capacity. Allow me to maintain a high vibrational offering so that I can consciously and intentionally feel the Universe work through me. Help me to remember that I am always a bright light shining and if ever I feel anything other than that, it is me just dimming my own light. Remind me that true gratitude is embodying the love that I am and sharing that love with the world. Thank you for guiding me to new heights and revealing the path that has always been within me. And so it is. Amen.

So what is the deepest truth of all…? Love is all. I once had a client who was in a deep meditation, and she asked for an answer. And was expecting profoundness. On our call, she was telling me what message she had received. She said "all they told me was that I am love, and I was expecting more than that". I paused for a moment. And I said, "ok, let's say the message was something else, something tangible. You would apply the tangible experience, you would learn a lesson from it, you would peel back the layers, just to eventually realise the ultimate truth, which is that you are love. So God gave you the most profound realisation of all. THE truth." It's safe to say that her perspective shifted after that. But that's often what humans do. We over-complicate the simple truth. Love is all. Period. We want more. We want to know what sort of love, how do we apply that love, does that love have a purpose, how do we find that purpose, why don't we always feel the love (hint: we resist it), does that love define the path, etc. And we replace the word love with millions of things. But ultimately we want to understand ourselves better, and now that we know for certain that we are love, it's clear that we want to understand love better. But none of those questions matter, because the answer is absolute. Love is all. How that love is projected, felt, evolving, expanding and transmuting is the beauty of the human condition. We have free will. It is the design. We want love to be both dynamic and absolute. And here's the kicker, it is. We are the channel of that ever-evolving, ever-expanding, yet absolute love.

-

Do our soul's choose which body we will move into each lifetime? I struggled knowing what felt like the truth with this for a long time. I would move in and out of the idea that we choose our lives. But now I am certain that we do... We choose the best possible vessel, the best possible soul cluster (our family, friends, significant people in our lives), the place we will be born and even some of our soul journey, based on what is the most conducive for the expansion we wish to experience in this lifetime. There are soul contracts that come with us also, based on past lives and soul journeys, however free will reigns and we can make conscious decisions in the 3 Dimensional to not live them out, however if we do this, they will come with us into our next lifetimes until we have moved through them. We plant seeds in every lifetime, that if nurtured come with us for every lifetime that follows. This explains why some experience their awakening at an earlier age, because they had learnt so much in past lives, that the carbon copy (memory) of the lessons surfaced faster. Recently a friend of mine came across a mystic in Sri Lanka, and the mystic revealed that skills that we Master in each lifetime come with us into the next. So learn as many skills as possible. I believe that the resonance lives on forever, because it is just energy, and if I master it in this lifetime, it will be closer within reach in every lifetime. Now to be clear, EVERYTHING is within reach, but my soul is retrieving from past personal experience and not the collective consciousness, making the imprint of it more familiar. I've shared elsewhere in this book that once a psychic friend of mine, did a reading on me and revealed that "I know the unknown", and I truly believe it's because I mastered it in past lives. I have done many past life regressions and seen myself as High Priestesses, Deities (yes they are real), witches, Sirens, a medicine woman, and so many other enchanting life experiences, and with each lifetime, I learnt so much about mysticism and esoteric teachings that naturally they would come with me in this lifetime. And as I am writing this now, I am channeling, and maybe I am not channeling from the collective consciousness after all, maybe I am channeling from the lessons I've learnt in my past lives (which of course is of the collective consciousness), who's to say really. And of course it doesn't matter, because this information was going to come through regardless of where it came from. But in the pondering, I am expanding, and as I plant these seeds in this lifetime, and Master the lessons, I will bring in so much realised wealth into my next lifetime. And notice I said "realised", because the wealth (abundance, or whatever else you want to call it) is ever present, but the realisation is often what people struggle with. And by struggle, I mean resist. Because that's all we are ever really doing, aligning or resisting alignment.

-

Recently I was meditating and this question came into my awareness; "if as spirit I don't have a conscious mind, how do I "choose" to come into physical form?". I was then clearly instructed that it has to go into this book. I will share a basic understanding here, but I will dive deeper into this topic in my next book.

We are of one collective mind with a universal intention to expand. Parts of you are always choosing to expand in physical form. Whichever is most serving for the best expansion experience.

That's why different parts of the one collective mind (aka "souls") choose certain times and spaces to come into physical form. We always have other intentions in other planes. But the physical plane is for expansion.

I should add that it's not so much a conscious choice as it's the natural order, let's call it evolutionary to help with the understanding. A form of sacred encoding. The same way that dogs instinctively know to chase cats.

As mentioned elsewhere in this book, time is not linear. The intention was the vibrational frequency of the physical form waiting to be realised. And that intention magnetised the spirit to the physical experience. The intention (to expand) materialises in all dimensions and forms.

Ponder this thought, are we planting seeds of desire in the present, to come to the realisation of that intended desire in physical form later, or is it also possible that future you is looking out for present you by planting seeds of desire to be focused upon, because it knows in the realisation of them (they have already been realised, think of time as a circle) you are on your most aligned path...?

-

As I'm almost at the end of my writing of this book, I've been asking for "final thoughts" from Source. And here's the thing... I asked for more revelations and what I was told was that there is no more you need to know right now. You have all that you need. And in fact, too much information can become destructive, because it can become all consuming. So instead everything you need has already been revealed and when you are ready for more, more will become realised by you. Even if I were to tell you more now, you wouldn't have any use for it, because it can't be applied until we understand the layers already presented. Love is all and all is love. And beyond that, there's nothing more you need. And this is a collective understanding. I'm aware that some can know more, and that's because they are ready for this. But for you, who are here right now, reading this, this is all for you. Take what you know, intuitively, and do not be afraid to act on that intuitive guidance.

The other thing I will add about seeking information (that can be destructive and of the ego, when coming from a place of separation and lack from the all-knowing Source); all things, all knowledge, everything that exists in the collective consciousness, is accessible to you. So even the people you follow, the books you read, the programs you sign up to, and the stimuli you absorb, can all be accessed when you silence your conscious mind and ask God. The revelations are ever present, and whatever is in alignment with your personal soul journey will be realised by you. So even if you don't sign up to the course, what lessons you need from that course can come to you anyway. Often the book, course, talk, podcast, movie, or whatever it is, has come from an intuitive nudge, God's way of directing us to the answers we seek. But self-awareness will allow us to know if it is coming from an intuitive place or it is coming from a destructive place, where we seek more because we feel that we don't have enough, or we seek more to externally validate, or we seek more to escape. Check in with yourself to understand your intention for more information.

And if all of this (the human experience) was to end, you do not need to worry, as I (you and all of us) have returned to the stars that I (and we) came from.

And so it is.

ABOUT THE AUTHOR

GRIGORIA KRITSOTELIS

Grigoria, Spiritual Teacher and Mindset Coach. She is dedicated to raising the vibration of the earth by spreading the message of light and love.

Grigoria has mastered her craft in the Spiritual arena and applies spiritual practices to all her teachings. She is a thought leader, creative intellect and has a magnetic light-filled energy that demands the attention from any room she enters. She has used these skills to speak on stages, host retreats and events, and create hundreds of training content to serve her audience. Her focus is on creating a sacred safe space for people to reconnect with their true selves, remove their limiting beliefs that come from misguided thoughts and teachings and return to a state of alignment with the vibrational frequency of love.

Grigoria isn't just a teacher of spirituality, she embodies the light-filled energy she teaches and commits to sharing her knowledge on reprogramming the subconscious mind so that everyone can consciously live a life they desire.

A message from Gee

My goal in life is to be one of those people who are just light. You see them and you suddenly feel so warm inside, and all you want to do is hug them. And they look at you and smile with the warmest light in their eyes... and you love them. Not in a romantic way, but you just want to be close to them and you hope some of their light transfers onto you.

www.grigoriakritsotelis.com

CPSIA information can be obtained
at www.ICGtesting.com
Printed in the USA
LVHW051013110621
689905LV00012B/1663